AF560762

EUROPEAN CEMETERIES IN SOUTH INDIA

EUROPEAN CEMETERIES IN SOUTH INDIA

(*Seventeenth to Nineteenth Centuries*)

MARTIN KRIEGER

MANOHAR
2013

First published 2013

ISBN 978-81-7304-981-1

Published by
Ajay Kumar Jain *for*
Manohar Publishers & Distributors
4753/23 Ansari Road, Daryaganj
New Delhi 110 002

Typeset by
Kohli Print
Delhi 110 051

Printed at
Salasar Imaging Systems
Delhi 110 035

Contents

Tables

Illustrations

FIGURES

PLATES *between pp. 96–7*

Preface

This volume is the outcome of a research project I conducted between 2003 and 2005 at the University of Greifswald, Germany. It is with great pleasure that I recollect the countless days I spent on the subcontinent roaming across forgotten cemeteries between Masulipatnam and Kotagiri or visiting the beautiful churches between Madras, Tranquebar and Cochin. Several of my colleagues, friends and my family have supported this study—mentioning all of them would cover too much space. However, I am especially indebted to Prof. Dr Michael North of Greifswald University, who has always supported my work with material funds as well as his vast experience. Dr Alexander Drost joined the research project and helped to collect a bulk of relevant material, which has been invaluable for completing this book. Prof. Dr Jeyaseela S. Stephen (Shantiniketan), Dr Jean Deloche (Pondicherry), Prof. Dr Thomas da Costa Kaufmann (Princeton) and Prof. Dr Marten Jan Bok (Amsterdam) supported my project by sharing their broad knowledge with me. I would also like to extend my thanks to the staff of the British Library and India Office Records collections at London and to the Danish National Archives at Copenhagen, especially to Dr Erik Gøbel, whose kind assistance has always been of tremendous help. For about a year, the Nilgiri Library at Ootacamund was a kind of second home for me, where I enjoyed a lot of help, notably from Ms Daphne Sampson and her colleagues. Maria Moynihan (Greifswald) and Peter Bailey (Coventry) put in great efforts to correct my English and Saskia Helgenberger (Kiel) created the index. My publisher Ramesh Jain always encouraged me to complete this book and offered his generous assistance in helping to copyedit this volume. I am extremely indebted to the German Research Council (Deutsche Forschungs-gemeinschaft) for providing financial support to this project. The greatest thanks, however, go to Nimmy, Benny and Paul, who were forced to share my passion for old, crumbling tombstones through many years and always yielded a perfect environment to carry out my research. Without them, this book would not have seen the light of day.

Kiel
May 2012

MARTIN KRIEGER

Introduction

'Death was always our near companion'.[1]—These simple words from Rudyard Kipling's autobiography contain a universal truth experienced by countless Europeans who lived and served in the Indian subcontinent prior to India's Independence. A verse from Kipling's 'The Naulakha' provides an insight into the colonial perception of death in India as well:

And, the end of the fight
Is a tombstone white
With the name of the late deceased
And the epitaph drear:
A fool lies here
Who tried to hustle the East.[2]

Even if we do not share Kipling's views concerning the supposed foolishness of the Europeans east of Suez, his words are nevertheless apposite to our study. Death was indeed a 'near companion' in colonial India. Aspirations to make a fortune or to convert the 'heathen' were very often thwarted by deadly tropical diseases, accidents or melancholy, which in many cases inevitably lead to death or suicide. Most European men died while still in their twenties or thirties, while only a few one lucky survived to reach fifty. For women, the figures were even more dismal. Their children who were born here had a meagre chance of surviving their first year. While life expectancy rose steadily in Europe during the Early Modern period, it remained dismally low in colonial India. The numerous European cemeteries that survive in India and an even larger number of tomb monuments bear witness to this dark side of a supposedly glamorous life on the subcontinent.

People usually commemorated the deceased in private memory. Moreover, the creation of a suitably grand monument with an appropriate inscription was also an expression of European colonial and imperial power. As long as a memorial existed, the memory of the deceased prevailed. However, not everyone could afford to erect a monument in memory of the deceased. Commemoration thus depended solely on the social status and income. This kind of visual memory was not confined to cemeteries alone. In areas where there were no Christian burial grounds, monuments can be found along the roadsides throughout India. Where neither a burial ground nor enduring material for a monument was available, a simple tree sufficed. In 1755, for instance, whilst roaming on Nancowry Island, which is part of the Nicobar Islands chain, a group of Danish sailors came upon a weather-beaten inscription on a palm tree which bare the words 'Johan Willers 1725'.[3] Could this be the burial place of a sailor who had died exactly three decades earlier?

The palm tree on Nancowry Island has probably vanished now, but even so, thousands of sepulchral monuments in India survive till today and these still constitute an eminent element of the material culture of colonial South Asia. An investigation of these artefacts is not only rewarding for the historian of the colonial era, but it is a matter of urgency as well: The life span of the supposedly eternal inscriptions on granite slabs and even more so of brick edifices is limited. The tropical climate with its abundant rainfall, lush vegetation, peoples' need for land, neglect and vandalism regularly takes its toll on them.

The destruction of European burial grounds predates Independence. Records regularly contain reports on the neglect and decay from the beginning of eighteenth century—be it through complaints about noise and filth caused by grazing horses and alcohol vendors on St. Mary's Cemetery in Madras or about the deliberate neglect of an old Dutch cemetery belonging to the seventeenth century in Pulicat by the British authorities. After Independence, lack of funds meant that the fate of a large number of smaller burial grounds was legally sealed by an agreement between the Indian government and the British High Commission to let them 'revert to nature'. Today, the condition of the remaining cemeteries varies. Some are well-maintained thanks to the efforts of pastors and church authorities or the Archaeological Survey of India (ASI). Others are not cared for at all or have been deliberately destroyed, like the eighteenth-century Christ Church Cemetery in Cuddalore, whose monuments were removed during the 1990s—doubtlessly a severe loss to the town's heritage.

A historian writing a book on cemeteries in India must thus pursue three goals: In addition to making use of the surviving cemeteries, monuments and related archival sources for historical research, he or she has to record the present condition of the monuments for comparison at a later time. Finally, there is the hope that such a book would attract the attention of the public, doubtlessly, which are the best means of preserving the surviving cemeteries.

Against this backdrop, the present study investigates death and colonial cemeteries in south India between the seventeenth and the nineteenth century. The border drawn between the north and the south of colonial India for the purposes of this book may be arbitrary, but the enormous amount of material prevents a holistic perspective. Broadly speaking, the geographical focus will be on the current states of Andhra Pradesh, Tamil Nadu, Kerala, Karnataka and Goa. This largely resembles the area covered by the nineteenth-century Madras Presidency, Travancore, Mysore as well as the adjoining Portuguese, French and Danish possessions. Even for this more restricted focus, an encyclopaedic survey is by no means possible. On the contrary, representative examples will be chosen to illustrate major trends in burial culture and perceptions of death. The same applies to the temporal frame from the rise of the northwest European trading companies to the end of the Victorian era.

A European presence was established in India as early as the sixteenth century, and it lasted well into the middle of the last century. However, there is insufficient historical material relating to death in the first phase of Portuguese enterprise in the Indian Ocean, while sources on the twentieth century, especially the census and civil registration, by contrast, suggest an additional independent study with an entirely different, demography-based approach. The three centuries under scrutiny here nevertheless offer a broad enough spectrum of different nations, languages, religions and social classes to make them suitable for a comparative investigation.

Chapter 1 will utilize the material gained from the inscriptions as well as from archival sources to ponder demographical issues. To what degree do the extant sources render evidence on mortality-rate, age of death, infant-mortality and causes of death? These questions gain even more importance in view of the fact that almost no other sources besides sepulchral monuments and burial registers exist for the so-called 'parish register period' before the onset of civil registration. However, we have to consider that even this material has its limitations, for only very little information exists on migration within the colonial society, which might distort our figures.

Furthermore, the setting and structure of the European cemeteries in south India will also be examined (Chapter 2). The author of the present study hopes to have gathered a representative sample of European burial grounds. Many have been visited in person, others have been studied with the aid of archival and printed sources. Nationality and geographic location were the major criteria when choosing the cemeteries to be investigated. The sample includes burial grounds in former English/British, Portuguese, Dutch, Danish and French settlements, whereby a certain nation often represents a distinct religious denomination. At the same time, cemeteries from large towns (Madras) as well as from minor trading settlements, garrisons and hill stations were also chosen. To gain an insight into the significance and expressiveness of the material collected, the state of decay or conservation has to be scrutinized: How much is left of the original monuments? When did an obvious period of decay commence? This chapter will also endeavour to develop a typology of different cemeteries and reconstruct their chronological development. Several sample cemeteries will be studied with regard to their temporal development, and a horizontal stratification elaborated. This procedure will facilitate the reconstruction of the temporal development of the cemeteries and at the same time of the social distinctions made when interring people in different parts of a burial ground.

Insight into the structure and development of the cemeteries will facilitate the investigation of both the architecture and inscriptions of the monuments themselves (Chapter 3). However, before attention turns to such details, the process of their manufacture and erection will be studied. From the onset of the Dutch period in the seventeenth century, an industry developed around the production of stone slabs in India, and the country emerged as a leading exporter of these items to other parts of the Indian Ocean region. (India continues to export sepulchral monuments till today.) The question of the origin of the early sculptors cannot be solved satisfactorily. Only after the onset of the nineteenth century was the business of interring the deceased privatized, generating conditions for the rise of the private undertaker as a new profession in south India. Since records from these enterprises do not survive, their business activities can only be reconstructed with the aid of signatures on inscription plates, advertisements in local journals and with the help of records of the East India Companies. These sources offer a rough insight into the history of the undertakers, their products as well as the remarkable geographical range of their operations. Even for the modern observer, the transport of stone slabs weighing several tons, hundreds of miles overland, along slippery mountain paths up to the hill stations of the British Raj remains an astonishing feat. The most visible outcome of the stone masons', sculptors' and undertakers' activities are the countless sepulchral monuments that still survive in the European cemeteries of south India. The present volume endeavours to analyse their architecture and decoration in terms of shape and style: Can distinct forms of architecture be observed for a certain period or region? Did architecture and decoration mainly resemble the contemporary European taste or were hybrid forms of—for example—European architecture and Indian-style decorations created as well? Likewise, the investigation considers whether the architecture or the chosen materials yield evidence of the social status of the deceased. Similar questions also apply to the inscriptions. It has to be asked, whether an ever-changing perception of death generated distinct patterns of inscriptions. The most visible change, however, might be found in the abandoning of the Baroque 'memento mori'-image in favour of very individual expressions of mourning from the beginning of the nineteenth century onwards.

Nonetheless, the extant source material available for conducting research on death and colonial cemeteries in south India is not ideal. While an abundance of material exists for certain aspects such as architecture and the inscriptions of the monuments, the sources are silent on other aspects. This applies especially to the production of monuments during the seventeenth and eighteenth centuries.

The most important sources for the present volume are the cemeteries and the surviving monuments themselves. Of the several hundred cemeteries that still exist, about 20 were investigated for this study. One focus lies on the European trading settlements along the shores of the Indian Ocean. The major commercial centre of eighteenth- and nineteenth-century south India was Madras. Its modest beginnings after 1640 are reflected by the monuments from the original 'Guava Garden', which were later transferred to St. Mary's Church in Fort St. George. The surviving 'Guava Garden' stone-slabs are far outnumbered by those at St. Mary's Cemetery, which was founded close to the fort on the Island after the Seven Years' War. Other cemeteries, such as the extensive burial ground at Vepery, followed during the nineteenth century as the town expanded at an enormous pace.

While the British East India Company had founded its south Indian headquarters in Madras, other settlements emerged as the commercial centres of the competitors of the British. Already during the seventeenth century, the Dutch had settled in Pulicat, some 30 km north of Madras and in other smaller centres like Sadras and Nagapattinam. The headquarters of the Dutch Vereenigde Oost-Indische Compagnie (VOC) on the Malabar Coast were located in Cochin, after the town had been taken over from the Portuguese in 1663. Other minor factories in Malabar were subordinate to Cochin. The Portuguese were firmly settled in Goa and St. Tomé, south of Madras, while the Danes founded their commercial centre in Tranquebar and the French in Pondicherry. A number of trading settlements in Coromandel, such as Porto Novo (Parangipettai) or Masulipatnam, was not dominated by any single European trading nation, but these constituted quasi-international ports with factories belonging to different nations. Whilst some of these settlements had churches and churchyards, in others there were merely burial grounds next to the factories or at a safe distance to protect them from floods.

With the territorial expansion of the British East India Company in south India from the onset of the nineteenth century, other types of European settlements were established: the civil station and the military cantonment. Administrators, missionaries and merchants flooded into the hinterland of the newly-conquered territories. Even in formally independent states such as Travancore, British residencies were established and an ever increasing number of European troops was sent to India to safeguard the growing Empire. Many civilians and soldiers lost their lives in these places more due to diseases or accidents than war. New cemeteries had to be founded far inland and frequently extended.

Finally, the Europeans entered the mountains of the south, particularly the Nilgiris (Blue Mountains). From the 1820s, hill stations like Ootacamund, Coonoor and Kotagiri were established as recreational retreats for soldiers and civilians, but they soon emerged as towns in their own right. Here, the British and other Europeans found an environment that resembled their mother-countries. Clubs and libraries were founded, churches were erected and cemeteries built next to them.

The cemeteries studied in this book had been located and their extension documented. A list of cemeteries studied is given in Table 1. Furthermore, for selected cemeteries, monuments were photographed, measured, the remaining inscriptions were copied, and the position of the monuments within the precincts of the burial ground recorded. However, given the several thousand monuments, such a comprehensive approach was not feasible within the limits of this research project for the larger cemeteries, such as St. Mary's cemetery or the French burial ground in Pondicherry (Cholas Nagar).

Apart from the field data and archive material, this book has drawn on data relating to many more cemeteries from printed descriptions and anthologies. While the early anthologies such as the *Asiaticus* of John Hawkesworth (1803),[4] the *Complete Monumental Register* by M. De Rozario (1815)[5] or the *Oriental Obituary* of Holmes and Co.[6] focus specifically on Bengal, and others like

TABLE 1: LIST OF CEMETERIES STUDIED

Bimunipatnam, Flagstaff Cemetery
Bimunipatnam, Walanda Bhumulu
Cochin, St. Francis Church
Goa, Bom Jesus Cathedral
Kotagiri, European Cemetery
Madras, St. Mary's Cemetery (Guava Garden)
Madras, St. Mary's Cemetery (Island)
Madurai, St. George's Cemetery
Masulipatnam, Walandapalem
Nagapattinam, Karikop
Ootacamund, St. Stephen's Church Cemetery
Palakollu (monuments placed today in Vijayawada)
Porto Novo, Wannarpalaiyam
Pondicherry, Cholas Nagar
Pulicat, Binnenkerkhof
Pulicat, Buitenkerkhof
Sadras, Oude Kerkhof
Tranquebar, Gamle Kirkegaard
Tranquebar, Ny Jerusalems Kirkegaard
Tranquebar, Nyegade Kirkegaard

William Urquhart's *Oriental Obituary* (1809) offer a wide overview of India as a whole, the first anthology of tomb inscriptions from south India was published as late as 1905 by Julian James Cotton.[7] Even if this *List of Inscriptions on Tombs and Monuments in Madras* constitutes only a select list it offers an abundance of material for those cemeteries that could not be visited, and importantly, it provides an impression of a number of monuments that have been lost during the last century. The same applies for the collection of Dutch inscriptions published by Alexander Rea in the 'New Imperial Series' of the Archaeological Survey of India (1897).[8] A number of regional compilations of inscriptions published at the behest of the Secretary of State were a further resource for this study.[9] While there appears to have been little academic interest in cemeteries between the onset of the twentieth century and the first two decades after Independence, since the 1980s the British Association of Cemeteries in South Asia (BACSA) has published several compilations of inscriptions from British cemeteries in

India and beyond. Unfortunately only a few of these volumes deal with south India.[10] Only recently have the sepulchral relicts of other European nations formerly present in India been investigated. Two studies were of particular use for the present book. Besides exhaustive historical and philological investigations, the Dutch publication *In steen geschreven* by Marion Peters (2002) as well as the Danish study *Tranquebar* by Karin Kryger and Lisbeth Gasparski (2002) offer comprehensive collections of material on inscriptions.

The data collected on the cemeteries, on the inscriptions and on the architecture of the monuments constitute only one cluster of sources. The second comprises archival sources from the records of the European East India companies. First, the parish books of the European communities provide details regarding the profession of the deceased and the number of burials—to be compared with the number of remaining monuments. Unfortunately, further information such as the age of the deceased or the cause of death was only generally recorded from the onset of the nineteenth century. Data for the preceding centuries can only be roughly reconstructed. Additionally, infant and child mortality was studied using baptismal registers. Since an abundance of parish books survives, some selection is necessary. The present book thus mainly draws on the relevant records from Madras (St. Mary's Church)[11] and from Danish Tranquebar (Zion Church),[12] which date back to the end of the seventeenth and to the mid-eighteenth century respectively. The account books of Tranquebar's Zion Church have likewise been preserved and offer an excellent insight into the costs of burial between 1781 and 1817.[13] In many other instances, the records are not complete, papers have been destroyed or the accessible microfilms are of poor quality, so that it is often prohibitively difficult to collect comprehensive material for longer time periods.

Since the church and cemetery authorities were tightly connected with the East India Companies or were subordinate to them, an investigation of company records likewise seems to be rewarding. The large number of last wills offers an insight into the preparation for death, especially in a financial and material perspective.[14] After disbanding the local vestries in the Madras Presidency in 1805, the company-administration was also in charge of clerical affairs which generated a large amount of correspondence and minutes also on the British cemeteries, today preserved in the *Ecclesiastical Consultations* of the Government of Madras for south India.[15] A more recent stock of material was collected by the British High Commission in New Delhi during the first two decades after Independence, which had been entrusted with the care and future fate of the formerly British (and partly also Danish and Dutch) cemeteries.[16] This book does not at all claim to have investigated all available archival sources comprehensively, a task that would be unrealistic even as a lifelong enterprise. Nonetheless, it is hoped, that the material offered here leaves a representative image of the tangible and intangible culture of death in colonial south India.

NOTES

1. Kipling, *Something of Myself*, p. 42.
2. Quoted after Wilkinson, *Two Monsoons*, p. 195.
3. Archive of the Moravian Brethren, Herrnhut (UAH), R15 Ta No. 1.7, Reiß Diarium, 1755–1756, 22 November 1755.
4. Hawkesworth, *Asiaticus*.
5. De Rozario, *Complete Monumental Register*.
6. Holmes and Co., *Bengal Obituary*.
7. Cotton, *List of Inscriptions*.
8. Rea, *Monumental Remains of the Dutch East India Company*.
9. See individual annotations in this text.
10. The following BACSA publications exist on the cemeteries in the south: Munnar (Cooke), Bimlipatnam (Cooke), Vizianagaram (Cooke), Vizagapatnam and Waltair (De Jong), Quilon and Trivandrum.
11. India Office Records (IOR), London, N/2, Ecclesiastical Returns Madras, 1698–1947.
12. Landsarkivet for Sjælland, Lolland-Falster & Bornholm, Copenhagen, Sogn Nr. 777, Tranquebar Zions Kirkebog, 1767–1845 (microfiche).
13. Danish National Archives, Copenhagen (RA), Asiatisk Kompagni 1770a, Zions Kirkes og fattigkasses regnskaber 1781–1817.
14. IOR, L/AG/34/29, Madras Wills, Administrations and Inventories.
15. IOR, P/333, Madras Ecclesiastical Consultations.
16. IOR, R/4, British High Commission Cemetery Records *c.* 1870–1967.

CHAPTER 1

Death in Colonial South India

MORTALITY

The surviving monuments on the European cemeteries in south India constitute not only an eminent art historical source, but they also provide evidence of people's age at the time of his/her death. Thousands of inscriptions inform us of the exact date of peoples' deaths and their ages. This chapter investigates the issue: to what degree does the information gleaned from the monuments contribute to demographical investigations, notably to studying the average age of death? While the bulk of demographical studies in rural and urban Early Modern Europe already exists by making use of parish books, the tremendous mobility of the colonial society prohibits similar investigations in India. Only a small percentage of Europeans died in the same place where they were born, so a comparison between baptism, marriage and burial records is futile. On the other hand, the age of death is mentioned in the parish books only from the onset of the nineteenth century, as an investigation of the entries from St. Mary's Church, Madras, and from Zion Church, Tranquebar, reveals.[1] A statistical investigation, even for the periods after 1800, proves to be problematic, since the so-called 'parish register period'—i.e. the time before the introduction of civil registration—imposes enormous problems in the determination of mortality rates from the relevant sources.[2] Furthermore, the number of migrants among the colonial society is not known. Complaints about a slack administration of the records were frequent, especially for the period around 1800.[3] Under-registration of births and death of infants was quite common in Europe and in colonial India as well.[4] Many sources seem to provide comparatively weak data for statistical investigation, and the registers themselves must be investigated with great caution.

We thus have to ask if the demographic material gained from the cemeteries is a reliable source complementing the data from the parish-books? Against this backdrop, it has to be taken into account that only a small share of the deceased was commemorated by erecting a monument with a surviving and still legible inscription tablet. While, for example, the burial registers of St. Mary's Church record 23,334 funeral services during the period 1763–1899, only 521 inscriptions could be found and analysed in this cemetery for the same period, which equates to a mere 2.2 per cent. The ratio proves to be slightly better for Danish Tranquebar, where 816 recorded funeral services are to be compared with 57 surviving inscriptions from the period between 1767 and 1845 (7.0 per cent). At the same time we have to consider, that the number of deceased commemorated with a tombstone represents by no means the entire colonial society. More likely they had belonged to the social elites or the middle class especially during the nineteenth century. A sailor or soldier hardly had a monument erected in his honour in colonial India.

To gain at least a rough answer to our question, we may calibrate the inscriptions of the monuments (Figure 1) against the entries in the burial registers after 1800, when the age of death is mentioned in the records (Figure 2). St. Mary's Cemetery in Madras proves to be the best example due to the large number of surviving monuments. An investigation of these monuments for the period 1800 to 1849 clearly shows that child mortality for persons below 10 years proved to be comparatively high (21.9 per cent of all deceased). People who had successfully survived childhood had a good chance of surviving their youth (7.8 per cent for the life span 10–19). Most adults died during the twenties (22.8 per cent) to be followed by the thirties (17.4 per cent), forties (12.8 per cent) and fifties (11.4 per cent). Only a small proportion of the Europeans belonging to St. Mary's parish had the fortune to enter their sixties (3.7 per cent) or seventies (1.8 per cent). Becoming eighty years old was exceptional (0.5 per cent).

A comparison between Figures 1 and 2 clearly shows that the data largely resemble each other. Furthermore, the burial records provide evidence for the fact that a life span of between 10 and 19

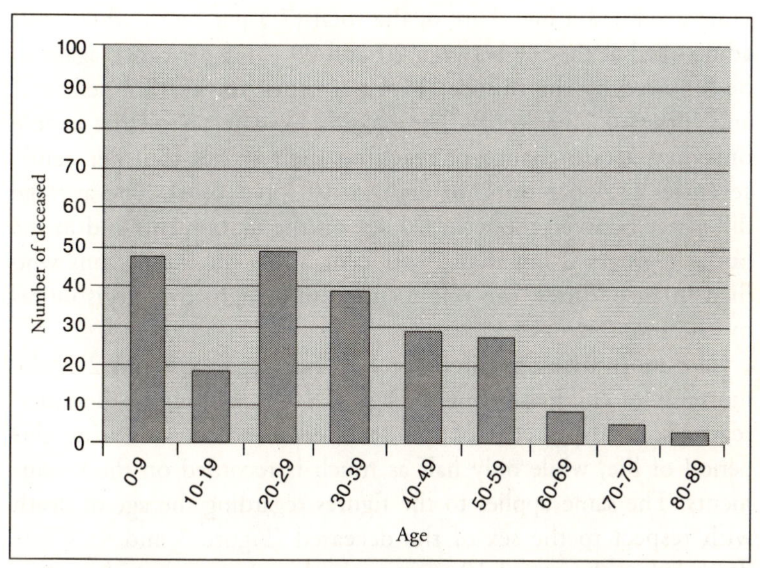

Figure 1: Age of death as recorded on the monuments at St. Mary's Cemetery, Madras (1800–49)

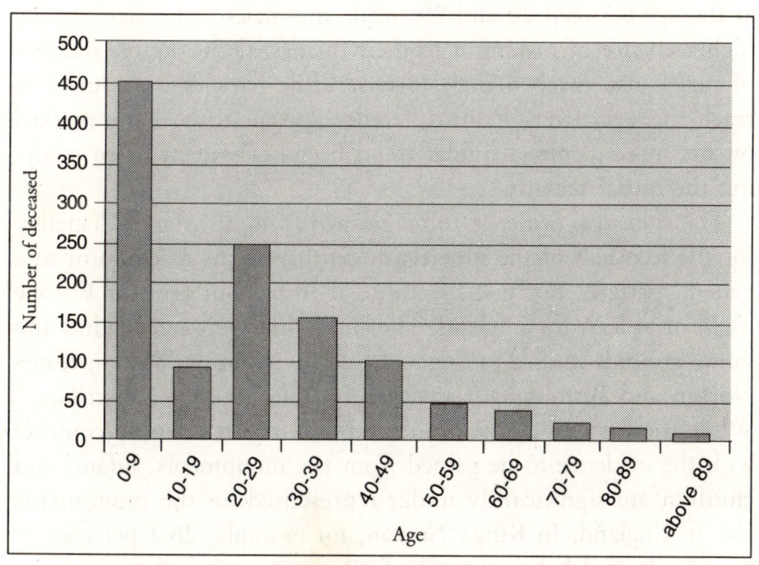

Figure 2: Age of death as recorded in the burial registers of St. Mary's Cemetery, Madras (1825–6; 1835–6; 1845–6)[5]

years exhibited a low share of the total (7.3 per cent), while most adults died at the age between 20 and 29 (21.5 per cent), again to be followed by the thirties (14.4 per cent), forties (8.7 per cent) and fifties (4.2 per cent). The records likewise reveal that people only had a rare chance of reaching their sixties (3.0 per cent), seventies (1.4 per cent) or eighties (0.3 per cent). The average difference between the recorded age on the monuments and in the burial registers is less than 2 per cent. Only for the persons who died in their fifties, can one distinguish a slight over registration by the monuments.

The most striking difference between Figures 1 and 2 is the mortality of children below the age of 10. According to the burial registers, 39.0 per cent of the deceased passed away during this period of life, while only half as much is recorded on the monuments. The same applies to the figures regarding the age of death with respect to the sex of the deceased (Figure 3 and 4).While death below the age of 10 years again does not prove to be representative, the data for the adults are quite well comparable. They reveal the fact that the highest mortality among females occurred at the age between 20 and 29, while the males had a significantly higher chance of making it to their thirties. Quite a large number of males also reached their forties, while females were lucky to reach this age. Even if this difference appears to be more marked on the monuments, a similar trend becomes evident when studying the burial records.

The statistical evidence to be gleaned from St. Mary's Cemetery for the first half of the nineteenth century seems to conform to a general pattern, not just for colonial India, but also for Europe itself, or at least for England. The similarities between Madras and burial grounds studied in England, such as Wootton Wawen, King's Norton and Birmingham analysed by Iola Shorters are striking.[6] While the data for adults from the burial registers largely coincide with the evidence to be gained from the monuments, infants and children are significantly under-represented on the monuments also in England. In King's Norton, for example, 26.2 per cent of the people died below the age of 10 years, compared to a meagre 7.3 per cent to be gleaned from the inscriptions.[7] We may thus

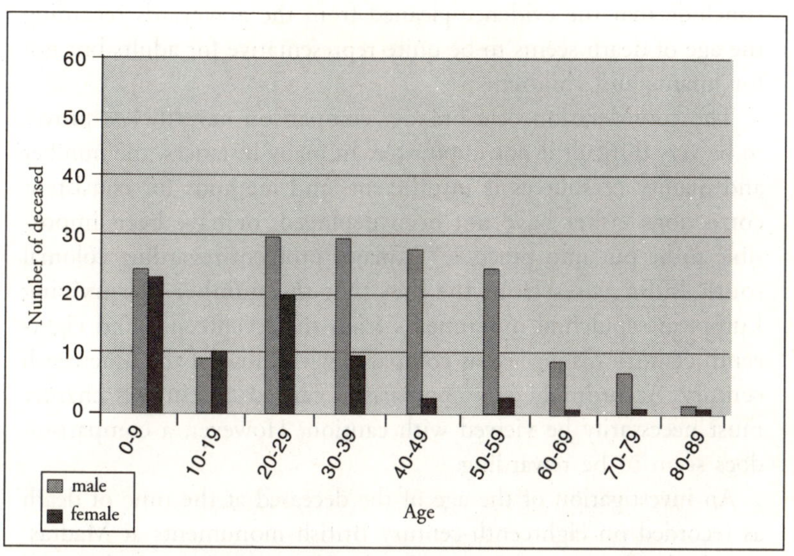

Figure 3: Age of death of males and females as recorded on the monuments at St. Mary's Cemetery, Madras (1800–45)

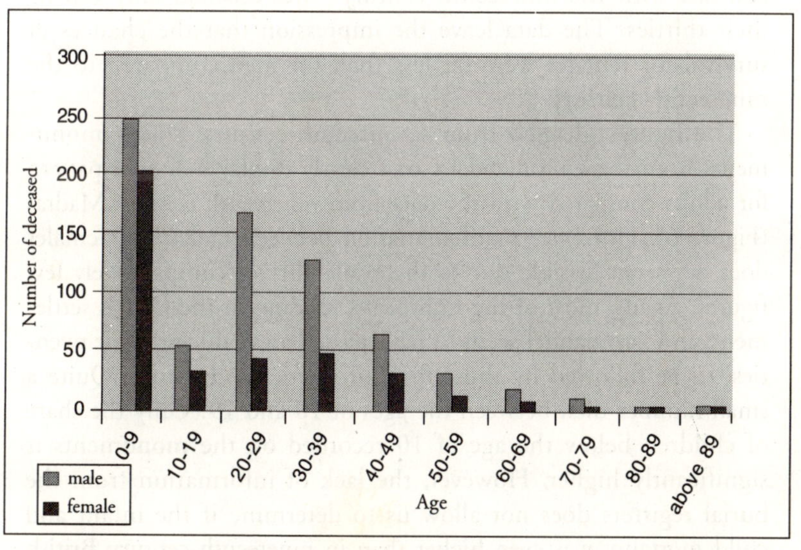

Figure 4: Age of death of males and females as recorded in the Burial Registers for St. Mary's Cemetery (1825-6; 1835-6; 1845-6)

conclude that the evidence gleaned from the graveyards regarding the age of death seems to be quite representative for adults but not for infants and children.

The consideration of a broader comparison nevertheless proves to be very difficult if not impossible. In many instances, the number and quality of sources is insufficient, and methods for consistent corrections either have not been deployed, or have been impossible to be put into practice.[8] A major problem regarding colonial south India arises from the fact that the number of surviving European sepulchral monuments from the seventeenth and eighteenth centuries is far less as compared with those of the nineteenth century. Accordingly, any comparison carried out in this chapter must necessarily be viewed with caution. However, a comparison does seem to be rewarding.

An investigation of the age of the deceased at the time of death as recorded on eighteenth-century British monuments at Madras[9] reveals the fact, that females who died between the age of 10 and 19 years far outnumbered the males (Figure 5). Again, most females died in their twenties, while the peak of male mortality—in contrast with the nineteenth century—was reached only during their thirties. The data leave the impression that the chances of survival for females were far less than for men compared to the nineteenth century.

The figures gleaned from seventeenth-century Dutch monuments from the Coromandel Coast clearly display a similar pattern for adults compared with the data from nineteenth-century Madras (Figure 6). However, a differentiation between males and females does not seem feasible due to the availability of comparatively few figures. Again, most of the Europeans residing in the Dutch settlements in Coromandel seem to have passed away during their twenties, to be followed by those in their thirties and forties. Quite a small number died between the ages of 10 and 19. Only the share of children below the age of 10 recorded on the monuments is significantly higher. However, the lack of information from the burial registers does not allow us to determine if the infant and child mortality was even higher than in nineteenth-century British India, or if a larger number of deceased children was recorded on the monuments.

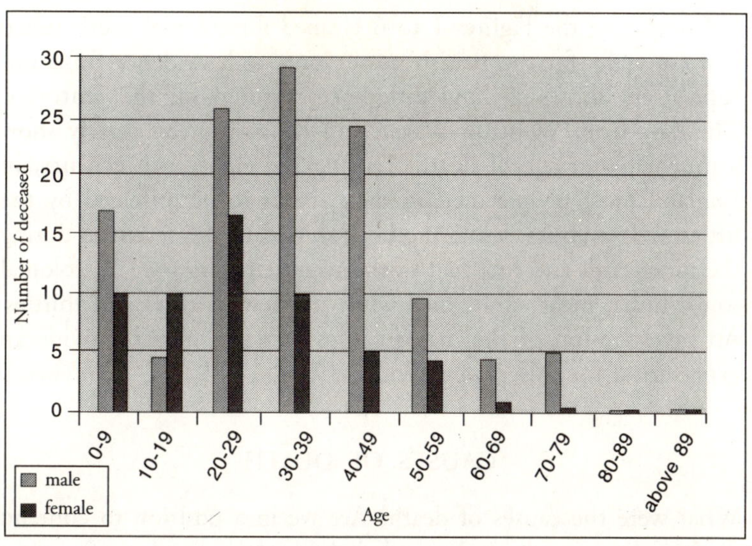

Figure 5: Age of death of males and females as recorded on the eighteenth-century British monuments in Madras

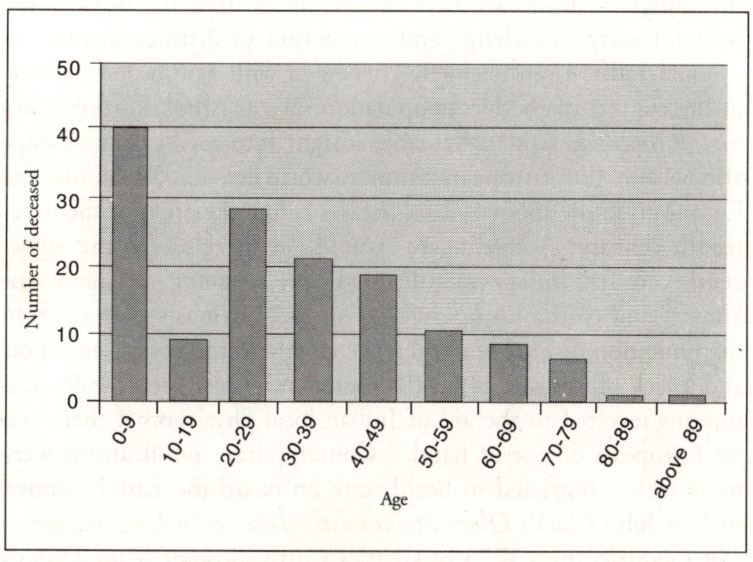

Figure 6: Age of death as recorded on seventeenth-century Dutch monuments in Coromandel

Comparing the Figures 1 to 6 gleaned for colonial south India, and especially for the British possessions, with evidence from Europe itself, shows striking differences throughout the centuries. The data from Wootton Waven and King's Norton clearly show a much higher age of death. During the eighteenth century, in England most people died in their sixties to be followed by the fifties and seventies, while the peak shifted to the seventies during the nineteenth and first half of the twentieth century.[10] In colonial south India, most adults died while in their twenties and thirties. An investigation of the major causes of death might provide an explanation for this phenomenon.

CAUSES OF DEATH

What were the causes of death? Are we in a position to contend distinct diseases which demanded the highest number of victims among the colonial population in south India? Because the author of the present study is no physician, any observation may be erratic and does not claim to be comprehensive. When investigating the causes of death, we first and foremost need to consider the contemporary knowledge and perception of distinct diseases in colonial India. Even if chiefly concerned with European medicine in the context of the local population, David Arnold's study *Colonizing the Body* renders valuable insight into medical knowledge also within the European colonial world itself.[11] What did the Europeans know about Indian diseases before the onset of the nineteenth century? According to Arnold, 'at the close of the eighteenth century, India was still, medically speaking, a largely unknown land to the Europeans'.[12] This fact obviously derived from the limitation of European presence chiefly to the coastal entrepôts and a lack of knowledge on the hinterland. Only incidentally, Europeans reverted to the aid of Indian local physicians if there was no European doctor at hand.[13] Contemporary publications were more or less restricted to health care on board the East Indiamen such as John Clark's *Observations on the Diseases in Long Voyages to Hot Countries* from 1773 or Charles Curtis' *Account of the Diseases of India, as they Appeared in the English Fleet, and in the Naval*

Hospitals at Madras, in 1782 and 1783 from 1804. According to Arnold, only the study on *The Influence of Tropical Climates, More Especially the Climate of India, on European Constitutions* by James Johnson (1813) broadened this quite narrow, maritime view towards medical issues of the tropical land itself.[14] However, in contrast to Arnold's observations, we may contend, that a limited European interest in Indian medicine indeed existed even from the outset of the eighteenth century, which, for instance, originated from the ethnographical studies of the German missionaries from Halle. Gründler's (however, unpublished) *Malabar Medicus* may be considered as the most prominent outcome of these efforts.[15]

A systematization and professionalization of European medical knowledge about the tropics only took place during the first decades of the nineteenth century—an observation that very well corresponds to the increasing accuracy of the entries in the burial registers at St. Mary's, Fort St. George, which constitute our main source for this chapter. It were chiefly the 'medico-topographical' surveys from the 1820s onwards, which brought forth a more specified knowledge on the most relevant diseases in a spatial context.[16] Three types of diseases were now regarded as the most life-threatening ones: fevers (later chiefly to become known as malaria), and liver and bowel diseases, especially cholera, which was soon perceived as the most dangerous disease to the Europeans as well as Indians and was widely discussed from these times. Non-epidemic diseases were obviously less investigated in the nineteenth century.[17]

A look at the sources, especially the burial registers of St. Mary's, at first leaves the impression that not only distinctly tropical diseases demanded a high toll, but also a very broad spectrum of general illnesses, which were common in Europe too. St. Mary's burial register of 1846, for instance, mentions the following causes of death, with the number of deceased: dysentery (30), cholera (27), convulsion (20), fever (11), dentition (10), dropsy (9), hepatitis (5), diarrhoea (4), consumption (4), childbirth (3), catarrh (2), cold (2), fractures (2) and leprosy (2). Only one victim each is recorded for brain fever, tetanus, mesenteric fever, paralysis, infirmity, water in the chest, sore throat, milk wash, affection of the chest, apoplexy, delirium tremens, drowning, spleen, hydrophobia, phtises, atrophia, epilepsy, affection of the heart, rheumatism, smallpox and inflammation of the bowels. Astonishingly only two persons presumably died of 'old age', while dentition and convulsion prove to be specific children's diseases instead.

Studying this impressive list, even the non-physician might presume that a proper and clear diagnosis was not always given. Usually the clerics proved to carry out the entries in the burial-register, and a physician was not always at hand. Another fact which poses additional problems to our investigation is that the entries in the burial registers of St. Mary's record the causes of death only from about the 1820s, and even then, not for every year. Also the parish books of the Zion-Church from Tranquebar mention the causes only in very few instances and are thus not suited for a quantitative investigation. Any quantitative analysis will thus render only a coarse impression on the matter.

The most lethal diseases were obviously not the most widespread ones. Hull has listed the most common diseases in colonial India as dyspepsia, diarrhoea, cholera, dysentery, fevers, jungle fever, heat apoplexy or sunstroke, disease of the liver, prickly heat, boils, constipation, colics, convulsions, diseases caused by intestinal worms, accidents, bruises or sprains, hemorrhoids, burns, snake-bites, fractures, dislocations, drowning and poisoning, notably opium-poisoning. Some of them only rarely occur as causes of death in the parish books—not even 'fever', which we, to some degree, may identify as malaria.[18] Among the Europeans in south India, two diseases proved to be most fatal instead: dysentery and cholera.

Dysentery (or flux, body flux) is an intestinal disease which leads to severe diarrhoea and, if untreated, proves to be fatal. It is not a distinctly tropical illness, but it obviously occurs more often and severe under warmer climatic conditions. It is commonly (but not exclusively) caused by a bacterial infection. The most relevant form of treatment proves to be the replacement of the lost fluid. Dysentery was common among the European population in India and was thus described as 'one of the pests of hot climates'.[19] Its symptoms are described by Hull thus:

Severe griping pain, especially in the lower part of the bowels, increased on pressure; frequent evacuation of the bowels, with great straining, the stools being composed of mucus, or slime, and blood, or both together; the tongue is coated and foul, there is depression and generally some fever, and subsequently great prostration.[20]

Hull's observation, that 'it is more commonly met with and more destructive when there is a fall of rain after a long continued drought, as at the change in the monsoon, and a high temperature long continued predisposes to an attack', might be questioned against the backdrop of figures shown in Table 2.[21]

The figures clearly unveil the fact that death due to dysentery was only slightly unequally distributed throughout the year in mid-nineteenth century Madras ranging from an average of 1.6 to 2.3 victims per month. The dry months February, April, May and June witnessed the lowest death rate. The dry months of March and August as well as the rain-periods brought about a slightly higher likeliness to fall victim to dysentery. Distinct epidemics compared to cholera-epidemics cannot be traced from the sources. We thus cannot support Hull's observations on distinct periods with a higher chance to catch this disease.

Even if dysentery in the long run presumably claimed the highest toll in mid-nineteenth-century Madras, cholera was obviously felt to be more threatening by contemporary public opinion. The most terrifying aspect was its sudden appearance and the likeliness to be affected by it. These characteristics are extensively dealt with in Hull's *Anglo-Indian's Vade-Mecum*:

TABLE 2: NUMBER OF VICTIMS OF DYSENTERY AT ST. MARY'S, MADRAS, MONTHLY AVERAGE 1845–53

Month	Jan.	Feb.	March	April	May	June
Number of dysentery-victims	2.0	1.8	2.6	1.3	1.9	1.6

Month	July	Aug.	Sept.	Oct.	Nov.	Dec.
Number of dysentery-victims	2.3	2.3	2.4	2.4	2.0	2.3

Cholera is, without exception, the most dreaded of all diseases. Its invasion is so sudden, its course so rapid, and its fatality so great, that it is little wonder its appearance in any district should excite more or less fear and consternation. In some parts of India it is scarcely ever absent, and with very few exceptions no spot in the whole peninsula escapes its ravages during the year. In large cities and densely populated villages, where ordinary sanitary laws are disregarded,—in other words, where drainage and ventilation are bad,—the disease every now and then breaks out and spreads with great rapidity.[22]

Cholera is a bacterial infection. The germs are commonly spread through contaminated food or water. In contrast to dysentery, it can lead to wide-ranging epidemics. In 1818, the secretary of the Madras Medical Board exhaustively describes the symptoms of cholera:

It commences with a sense of heat in the epigastrium and slight watery purgins accompanied by a great langour and depression of spirits, with a diminished temperature of the surface of the body. The uneasiness at stomach and watery purging with a most remarkable prostration of strength increase rapidly; spasms are felt in the extremities, the pulse becomes very small and languid, and unless the symptoms are arrested by medicine, the vomiting and purging of a glary nearly colourless matter becomes more urgent—the cramp extends from the feet and legs to the muscles of the abdomen, thorax and arms—affecting those of a robust habit and in whom the attack is severe, with most excruciating pains, and exhausting the vital energies so rapidly that the patient in six or eight hours loses his pulse at the wrist; his body is bedewed with a cold clammy sweat, the eyes are dull and heavy, are covered with a film, occasionally suffused with blood and insensible to the stimulus of light, ...

Such initial symptoms are followed sometimes by 'insatiable thirst'. Soon death occurs: 'In this severe epidemic, death has hitherto been observed to ensue from 10 to 24 hours from the commencement of the attack.'[23]

A quantitative analysis of cholera epidemics in India proves to be problematic. Arnold deplores the lack of data for the times before the late 1860s. Even if they do not cover the local Indian, but only the European populace, the entries in the parish books of St. Mary's at Fort St. George render a narrow but elusive insight into this issue already from the 1840s. The burial entries notably inform us about the course of a cholera epidemic and the number of victims among the Europeans. We may thus contend a very distinct pattern: At times, the burial-registers do not record cases of cholera for many months. Next to these periods, epidemics with a high death-toll can be identified. An obviously severe epidemic during the period of the second worldwide cholera pandemic (1829–51) is to be witnessed starting from mid-1845 at Madras, which lasted until 1846.

Figure 7 depicts the development of this cholera epidemic during 1845–6. It started all of a sudden in mid-June 1845 and reached a climax only one month later with 20 victims during the latter half of July. By August the number significantly fell, but even them, the disease claimed 22 victims among the Europeans. Another (lower) climax was reached by January 1846 with 14 victims, while the epidemic died down only by February 1846, nine months after it first appeared in Madras. In the following months there were only a few cholera cases (one each in May, June, October and November 1846). For the subsequent decade, a series of

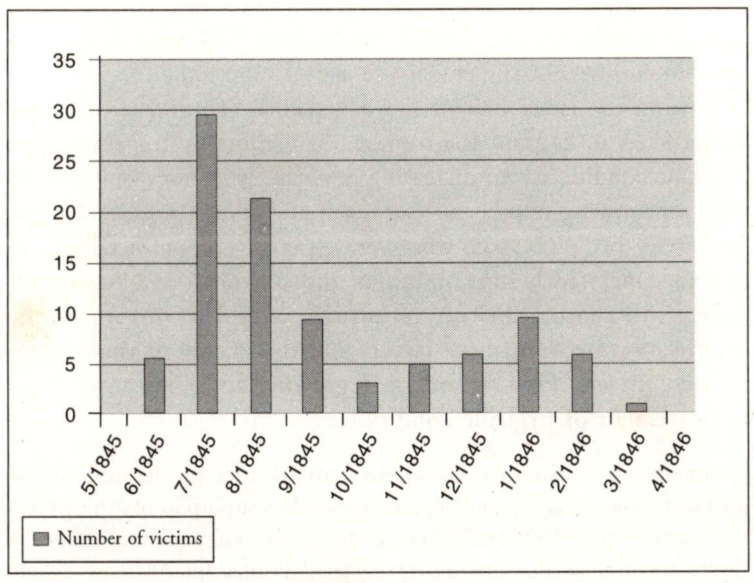

Figure 7: Recorded number of Europeans who were victims of cholera, St. Mary's, Madras (May 1845–April 1846)

cholera cases (however, to a much lesser scale) is recorded for March–September 1849 and January–August 1852.[24]

These observations correspond to the results of Arnold's study *Colonizing the Body* for the latter half of the nineteenth century and the beginning of the twentieth century.[25] According to the sources, the course of the disease similarly corresponds to Hull's observations on the sudden outbreak of the disease and the fact that it does not appear in any distinct season of the year. However, it contrast to Hull, we cannot contend, that 'it is scarcely ever absent', for we very well identify longer periods without any deaths being ascribed to cholera.

Cholera epidemics did not spare even prominent members of the colonial elites, such as Sir Thomas Munro (died 1827) and Sir George Ward (died 1860), two governors of Madras.[26] The inscriptions on the tomb-monuments display a growing public awareness on the importance of cholera as a major reason of death from the latter half of the 1820s, but especially during the 1840s. In St. George's Cemetery at Madurai, a number of deceased are distinctly mentioned to have fallen victim to cholera, such as Charlotte, the wife of C.G. Scott, 'who died on 7 March 1832 after a few hours illness of cholera' at the age of nineteen.

During the latter half of the nineteenth century, efforts were undertaken to contain the number of victims by improving the hygienic conditions. An increasing medical awareness resulted from the ever growing number of European and Indian soldiers in British service in South Asia, who were especially prone to fall victim due to congested living-conditions and malnutrition. From mid-nineteenth century, British authorities started to investigate the interrelation between those factors and the gravity of cholera epidemics. Already Hull reports on a growing sensibility towards an improvement of hygienic conditions:

> As soon as it is evident that cholera threatens a district, the drains should be attended to, not on any account opened merely for the purpose of stirring them up, but thoroughly flushed with water, alone or containing a quantity of Condy's fluid, or chloride of lime, or some equally good disinfectant. All houses should be whitewashed, and in the case of those in which even one single person has been attacked, the place should be vacated for a time, and the inmates sent

elsewhere at the very earliest possible opportunity, for the purpose of having the house thoroughly cleaned and purified by disinfectants.[27]

Good hygienic conditions and quarantine of the affected were deemed to be the most appropriate means.

The bad health conditions of the soldiers and an increasing awareness lead to a public debate in Great Britain, which can only be touched upon here. In 1864, Charles Dickens' journal *All the Year Round* embarked on this discourse with clear and critical words to the public:

As to water-supply, the usual pipes are the native men called bheesties, who draw it where they like, and bring it in their backs in skins. Sometimes the surface-drainage is gathered in tanks; and when one has learnt how the undrained earth is polluted, it seems hardly necessary to look further for causes of dysentery and cholera. Hyderabad says that no doubt its water 'swarms with animal life'. . . . At Bangalore, the Ulsoor tank, used for drinking, is the outlet for the whole drainage of a filthy bazaar, with a hundred and twenty-five thousand inhabitants. The commander-in-chief says, 'The disgustingly filthy nature of the source from which the water used at Bangalore is taken, has been brought to notice scores of times by me within the last four and a half years; but, as usual, nothing has been done.' Even the wells are impure from sewage. They are open, and 'when they get dirty they are cleaned'.[28]

Similarly disgusting were the sanitary arrangements inside the military barracks, in Dickens' words:

Arrangements for washing and bathing are no better. Indian barracks and hospitals are so expensive that every man costs thirteen pounds for his proportion of the house-rent . . . ; and yet in these costly barracks and hospitals the elementary notion of a basin, or a bath, or a drain-pipe to carry off used water, has hardly yet been entertained. Only two stations in all India—Madras and Wellington—have anything like lavatories or baths, with proper laying on of water and proper draining off, either in barrack or hospital. Refuse water is usually conveyed into an adjacent cesspit, where, with all other foul matter, it is expected to sink into the earth.[29]

Despite such an increasing awareness, the health conditions among the European troops only gradually improved, and still during the first half of the twentieth century, cholera threatened countless lives in India.[30]

Next to dysentery and cholera, famines also affected the mortality among the Europeans in south India, especially during the earlier periods of colonial enterprise. Even if quantitative figures are not available, we may well presume that an increasing number of deaths even among the Europeans during periods of food-shortage did not occur due to a lack of food within the colonial society but more due to diseases spreading in consequence of the famine. Severe crises regularly occurred within two or three decades—sometimes more frequently. The records reveal a great famine in Madras in 1686–7, when about a tenth of the local population perished.[31] The annual mortality among the Europeans simultaneously sharply rose from 20–30 during the preceding years up to 80–90 in 1687–8.[32] The same development is to be witnessed for the subsequent famine in 1718–19. Later during the eighteenth century, food scarcities or famines obviously had a much lesser or entirely no impact at all on the mortality rate among the colonial society. This development might resemble an increasing demographic independence of the colonial society in Madras in the context of a spatial segregation between Europeans and the local population during the eighteenth century. However, even here, any assumptions must be viewed cautiously, and further research is needed.

We have already noticed an above-average mortality of young women, which cannot be explained by the causes of death investigated yet. We may ask instead: to what degree did death during childbirth contribute to the comparatively high mortality of younger women? In Europe, the mortality of women aged between 15 and 49 years was significantly lower than that of men during the late eighteenth and the nineteenth century. And death in childbirth obviously did not play a statistically relevant role in Europe. Most studies confirm a figure of roughly 1 per cent for Central Europe.[33] Despite the fact that the set of data available for Madras is much smaller than for social communities in Europe, the figures display a strikingly different picture. The figure for Madras (St. Mary's Church) proves to be much higher as compared to the data gleaned for Europe and was 10.7 per cent for the years 1845–6.[34]

Death in childbirth claimed some prominent victims such as Jean Françoise Dupleix, daughter of the famous French governor,

Dupleix who died on 14 September 1744: 'Within a period of thirteen months and nineteen days from the date of her marriage, she was big with child, was delivered; and died. The infant also expired.'[35] Personal grief and sorrow are hidden behind these plain words of Dupleix's Dubash Ananda Ranga Pillai.

Apart from diseases, accident and suicide likewise constituted a smaller, but nevertheless significant share among the deceased. A frequent accidental incident was death by drowning. Not only sailors lost their lives and drowned off the coasts while handling sailing ships or smaller boats,[36] Europeans too lost their lives accidentally by falling into rivers or tanks. Even if the few figures available do not facilitate a statistical assessment, the sources never-theless suggest that the largest number of such accidents occurred during the rainy season, when river banks or tanks might have been hardly visible amidst the flooded land. In some instances, a jump into a cool basin, river or lake on a scorching summer day likewise proved to be fatal. In April 1826, Reginald Heber, the second Bishop of Calcutta, died while taking bath in a basin belonging to the Judge of Thiruchirapalli (Trichinopoly) during a visit there.[37] On the other hand, only extremely unfortunate men—such as Joseph Lancaster and John Stoughton on 11 November 1853 at Madras—were struck by lightning.[38]

Suicide was usually committed by shooting oneself or by hanging and only in a rare instance 'by leaning his breast at the point of a sword'.[39] Especially within the military quarters or smaller trading settlements without much entertainment thoughts of ending one's life were obviously quite common. In Danish Tranquebar, in 1797 one officer and a constable committed suicide within five days of each other.[40] The reasons for such incidents usually remain unclear. However, from William Puckle's diary from the 1670s, it was also alcoholism and subsequent delirium that lead to depression and unleashed destructive forces among the psyche.[41]

Sometimes it was not clear whether the deceased had actually committed suicide or if he or she had fallen victim to an accident or murder. Quite easily the deceased was declared as a suicide victim, possibly to avoid further investigations such as in the case of the private Edward Morlow from Secunderabad, who was 'brought to the Hospital the Morning dead from a gun shot wound through the Head'.[42]

Suicide was regarded as an offence against the worldly and clerical order, and clerical as well as military rites—in case the offender had been a soldier—were denied during funeral. Suicide victims were usually buried without the common rites or 'privately' buried, as mentioned in the British records.[43] The corpses were buried outside the cemeteries, or sometimes within a distinct 'suicide cemetery'.[44] However, a loophole was maintained open, when it was found the deceased had committed suicide 'in a fit of temporary insanity'—which meant, that he obviously had no mental control of himself. This rule rendered the opportunity to quite a large number of Christian burials of suicide victims, nevertheless sometimes it gave rise to objections. In one reported instance from 1848, military honour was denied even when a Christian burial already had been granted to a private of the British garrison at Bangalore. This incident without doubt put the local cleric in a position of discomfort:

> When the funeral reached the burial ground I [i.e. the cleric] observed that it was attended only by a carrying party of four men under charge of a Corporal, and that all those marks of respect prescribed by her Majesty's Regulation were withheld. Nevertheless acting upon the verdict of the Court of Request, I proceeded with the usual order for the burial of the dead, which was not followed by any of the military honors at the interment of the soldier.[45]

A comprehensive investigation on suicides in colonial India is still to be carried out and might render a new image to the supposedly easygoing life in the East.

The execution of death penalty obviously contributed only to a minor degree to the high mortality rate among the Europeans in south India. Even if the exact figures are difficult to find, most delinquents must have been deserted soldiers.[46] In 1739, for instance, a European was assassinated in French Pondicherry for an unknown reason: 'At 4 this afternoon, a European was marched in custody to the glacis, and made to kneel. Four soldiers then came forward, and simultaneously discharging muskets, which were loaded with double charges, shot the poor fellow dead'.[47] The assassination in the afternoon emerged as a virtual public incident.

INFANT AND CHILD MORTALITY

Infant and child mortality surpassed even the high mortality among adults. Only a few infants survived to reach the age of childhood; and even then, death demanded its toll in many instances. It is extremely difficult to gain accurate data on infant and child mortality in colonial south India prior to the first half of the nineteenth century. While the inscriptions on the monuments are not representative at all, civil birth registration did not exist, and an investigation of the clerical records is not easy. At the same time, questions regarding the mothers' nutrition, forms of breast-feeding, abortion, infanticide or neglect are impossible to answer for seventeenth- and eighteenth-century south India.[48] Additionally, according to Dyson's research, the British records also from the latter half of the nineteenth and the first half of the twentieth century reveal immense under-registration of births. Particularly female births were under-registered.[49] Such observation obviously seems to correspond to a global trend also, as mentioned by Thomlinson.[50]

An examination of the baptism records of St. Mary's Church, Fort St. George, supports such an image already for the eighteenth century. While 55.6 per cent of the newborn children recorded in the files were males, only 44.4 per cent proved to be female.[51] This ratio seems to be unnatural, since the biological difference between both sexes amounts to a maximum of 5 per cent. The ratio appears to be more balanced and realistic during the nineteenth century (ratio for the years 1845–9: 49.5 per cent, baptisms for males, 50.5 per cent, baptisms for females). However, the entries for funerals seem to be unbalanced still during the nineteenth century for children below the age of 10. The burial registers of St. Mary's Church show a surfeit of male burials at 54.8 per cent. It is not clear if such a bias derives from a higher mortality among boys or just from under-registration of girls.[52] The burial registers of the Zion Church of Danish Tranquebar are similarly problematic. While the ratio was quite balanced for burials during the period 1768–1800 (males 48.4 per cent/females 51.6 per cent), a striking bias favouring males is to be noticed for the subsequent decades from 1801 to 1845 (males 68.7 per cent and females 31.3 per cent). It seems obvious that this gap does not result from a sudden drop in girls' death rate, but is more likely due to under-registration.[53]

Nevertheless, an attempt will be undertaken here to offer at least a rough idea. As Table 3 shows, neonatal mortality was extraordinary high in Madras during the first half of the nineteenth century. Almost 40 per cent of the deceased infants below the age of two had died within the first month of their birth. Death during the day of birth was also not uncommon, such as in the case of the French governor Dupleix from Pondicherry (1742), who 'was blessed with a son. As soon as he was born, each ship in the reach fired a salute of twenty-one guns, and the church-bells rang peals for half an Indian hour. But the life of the infant was limited to this period and his soul then retired to the feet of God.'[54] While the second and third month still bore a larger risk of death, the subsequent months witnessed lesser mortality. The ninth to the twelfth month again bore a higher risk.

This pattern seems to resemble a general trend for eighteenth- and nineteenth-century Europe: The infants were not only prone to be affected by disease immediately after birth, but also during a second period after weaning, which was likely to occur from the eighth month. As Eva Labouvie, for example, contends for some West German regions, most infants died within their first month of life. A number of diseases such as smallpox, scarlet fever, convulsion, German measles and diarrhoea was basically the reason for this.[55] In England and Wales, the relevant nineteenth-century records largely mention 'other causes' (more than 60 per cent) as the major reason for neonatal death and only in some instances

TABLE 3: DECEASED INFANTS 1qo IN PER CENT
(ST. MARY'S, FORT ST. GEORGE, 1825–6, 1835–6, 1845–6)

0-1	1-2	2-3	3-4	4-5	5-6	6-7	7-8	8-9	9-10	10-11	11-12
38.1	4.5	3.9	3.4	2.6	3.9	5.6	5.1	7.8	8.3	7.3	9.5

Row 1: age in months; *Row 2*: percentage of all baptized infants deceased under 1 year.

any specific diseases.[56] Generally, the figures support Buettner's observation that the most common causes of neonatal death in India such as convulsions and dentition were identical with those in Europe, while distinctly tropical diseases played a minor (but nevertheless substantial) role.[57]

A detailed investigation is, however, not possible for periods earlier than the nineteenth century, because the burial records do not mention the age of the deceased. Another problem for the earlier periods arises from the fact that the relevant parish books usually record the date of baptism and not the date of birth; we are thus in a difficult position when studying stillbirths and the number of children having died before baptism and who thus never were recorded in the registers.[58] As the mortality rate proved to be extremely high during the first few weeks after birth, approaching the latter problem is of crucial importance for a further understanding of the limited data.

The records of St. Mary's Church will again be chosen as an example, because the relevant baptism registers date back as far as 1704. At first, the length of the period having elapsed between birth and baptism has to be studied to get an impression about the reliability of data on infant mortality in colonial Madras during the so-called 'parish register period'.

Figure 8 clearly shows that baptisms in many cases did not take place immediately after birth. In only one-fifth of the recorded 182 cases, baptism took place within a week, and only about half of the children was baptized within a month. Another fifth was carried to baptism service during the second month, while almost one-third of the children were christened during their third month and one-and-a-half years. An average baptism took place 57 days after birth, after about two months respectively.

However, we cannot conclude from this observation, that any estimate on infant mortality of infants before baptism proves to be futile. On the contrary, it seems as if many children were given baptism or at least baptism in extremis if its impending death became visible. The parish books of the Zion Church of Danish Tranquebar prove to be an excellent example, because baptisms in extremis were carefully recorded by the local clerics in the burial

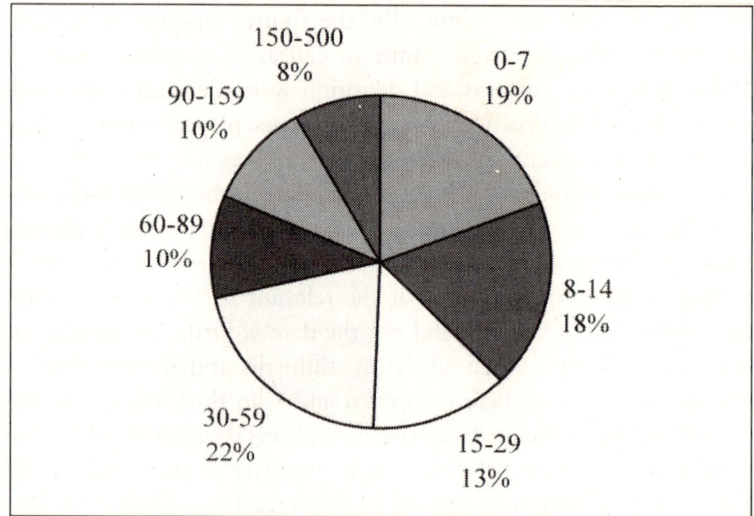

Figure 8: Period in days between birth and baptism, St. Mary's Church, Fort St. George (1728–53)[59]

registers. Between 1790 and 1839, the number of children buried in Tranquebar was 117, while 44 of them (37.6 per cent) had received baptism in extremis. On the other hand, only four children were buried without having been baptized, three among them being stillbirths.[60] Still born infants were buried without the usual rites, notably without the ritual deposition of earth on the corpse during the ceremony.[61] These data suggest (despite the statistical gap of about two months between birth and baptism), that at least in Tranquebar by far most of the deceased children had received baptism and were thus recorded in the burial registers.

Baptism in extremis was quite common in Europe as well as in colonial India. It could be carried out even in the absence of clerics. However, witnesses and a written proof were required to get the baptism being acknowledged by the church authorities and the baptism being recorded in the parish books. On 10 September 1801, for instance, an English soldier's daughter, Margaretha Chisolon, received baptism in extremis in Danish Tranquebar, which was at this time occupied by British troops in the course of the Napoleonic wars. The baptism was performed by Sergeant Major Archibald

M. Corquadall in the presence of Sergeant George Ballentin and a certain Mrs. Boss—all three names later being carefully recorded in the burial register.[62] In an unknown number of instances, baptism in extremis was also carried out by the father.[63]

Our observations allow us to gain at least some idea about infant and child mortality in colonial south India during the so-called 'parish register period'. Since data from St. Mary's parish records are incomplete or illegible for several years from 1744 onwards, one better focuses on the preceding decades.[64] Figure 9 shows the biennial number of baptisms and funerals of children who were born and also died in Madras between 1710 and 1741. The graph does not take mortality before baptism and migration into account and thus does not claim for absolute correctness of data. It rather intends to unveil a coarse trend and tries to show peak periods of mortality.

A low ratio between baptism and infant and child burials indicates a balanced relation between both figures, i.e. a comparatively low mortality and a larger number of baptisms. On the contrary, a large ratio expresses a lower number of baptisms coinciding with a raised mortality among infants and children. The latter might be an indicator of demographical crises—however, only to be seen on a micro-level according to the limits of the sources being consulted. On the whole, the graph shows a slight decline in the ratio throughout the three decades, corresponding to a better chance of survival, however, with enormous fluctuations and three peaks. The general downwards trend corresponds to the development of the Infant Mortality Rate (IMR) in England during the eighteenth century.[65]

The high mortality among children during the first peak rendered by Figure 10 corresponds to an exceptional high number of burials (including adults) between 1711 and 1713.[66] A second peak becomes visible for the biennial period from 1728 to 1729 with a slightly increased rate of burials and a much lower number of baptisms compared to the preceding years. This development coincides with a general scarcity in food supplies in Madras during 1728 and 1729.[67] An explanation for food shortage may be found in the fact that 1728 was a severe El Niño year with droughts

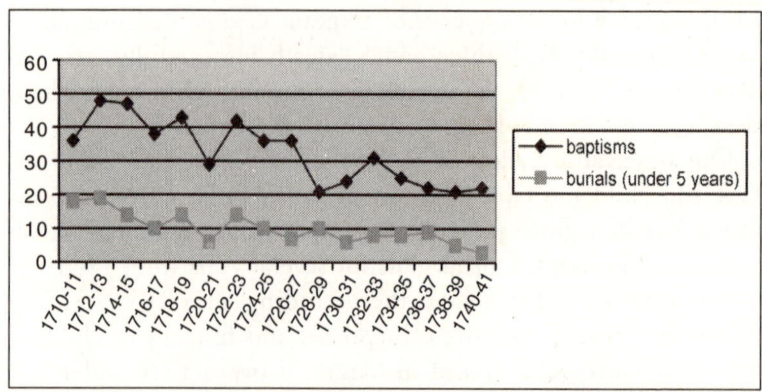

Figure 9: Number of baptisms and infant and child burials (of children being born and having died at Madras), St. Mary's Church, Fort St. George (1719–41)

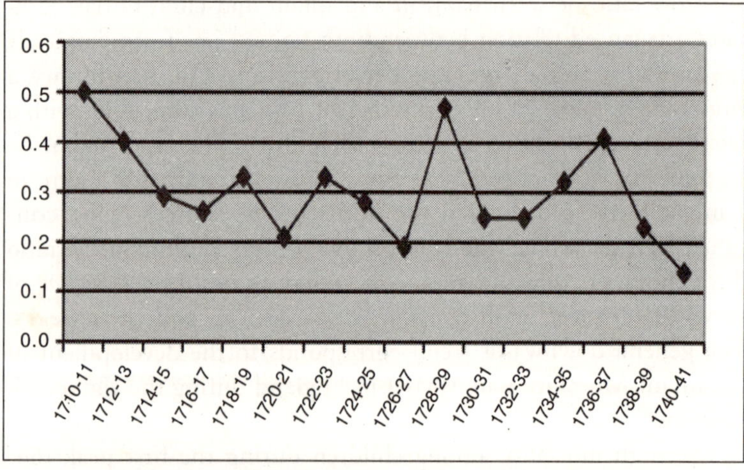

Figure 10: Ratio between baptism and infant and child burials at St. Mary's Church, Fort St. George (1719–41)

and a subsequent diminution of food supplies.[68] A second, however, weaker peak with a slightly increased mortality and a reduced number of baptisms similar to 1728–9 becomes visible for the biennial period 1736–7. It seems to impose no difficulties to relate this peak to a severe famine which took place in south India during 1737. Thanks to the weather diary of the German missionary Johann Ernst Geister of the period 1732–7 we are well-informed of the climatic condition of this period.[69] The data gained from this record reveal that the rainfall days throughout 1736 were much less than during the preceding years and that the months January to April 1737 were entirely rainless.[70] Geister writes on the year 1736:

> In the whole year there was little rain; until the end of the summer the landwind remained very strong and at the end of the year there was a large increase in prices. This aridity stretched from Madras 100 German miles northwards and over 10 German miles southwards, and quite a few day's journey inland.[71]

These observations correspond to the fact that 1737 again was a severe El Niño year with subsequent drought throughout large parts of the southern hemisphere.[72] Consequent to drought and nutrition-deficiency, people from the countryside flooded into Madras to seek relief.[73] It seems unlikely that the small European populace was struck by food shortage as well. We may presume instead that the children were less resistant against the health hazards resulting from rural exodus with its accompanying risk of common diseases and epidemics in the colonial town. However, both peaks—1728–9 and 1736–7—shall not be overestimated, since available data are limited.

Fluctuations in the mortality rate among children are not only to be observed throughout the years, but much more strikingly within the year, as for example the burial registers of St. Mary's Church unveil for the first half of the nineteenth century. The figures shown in Table 4 leave the impression of a changing mortality rate among children throughout the year. A peak in increased mortality can be observed between July and September—beginning two months after the occurrence of the highest average temperatures by May. It ends with the onset of the rainy season, which usually brings about cooler temperatures.[74] Interestingly, such coherence only to a much lesser degree applies to adults (see Table 5). As regards adults, the monthly death rate is more equally distributed between 6 and 11 per cent, which renders the impression that adults were less prone to be affected by seasonal changes of

TABLE 4: MORTALITY AMONG CHILDREN BELOW 10 IN MADRAS (ST. MARY'S CHURCH), ACCORDING TO MONTH, 1825–6, 1835–6, 1845–6 (IN PER CENT)

Jan.	Feb.	March	April	May	June	July	Aug.	Sept.	Oct.	Nov.	Dec.
5.9	5.7	3.4	5.9	6.4	5.9	12.3	15.1	15.6	6.8	8.1	8.9

TABLE 5: MORTALITY AMONG ADULTS (FROM 10 YEARS IN MADRAS (ST. MARY'S CHURCH), ACCORDING TO MONTH, 1825–6, 1835–6, 1845–6 (IN PER CENT)

Jan.	Feb.	March	April	May	June	July	Aug.	Sept.	Oct.	Nov.	Dec.
11.1	6.5	6.7	6.1	7.2	7.8	10.8	9.4	8.7	7.8	9.3	8.5

the climate. However, such interrelation between season and mortality rate among children was obviously not known to the contemporaries. Still in 1878, Hull writes in his *Anglo-Indian's Vade-Mecum*:

During the earlier years of life, that is till the age of seven or eight, European children, enjoy on the whole, as good health on the plains of India as they do in England. They are less liable to severe attacks of such diseases as scarlatina, diphtheria, measles, hooping cough, etc., and when they do suffer from them, the attacks and the secondary effects are generally much less serious, while the mortality is much less also.[75]

These words might have proved to be consoling to the parents, who probably did not have any choice other than bringing their children up in India, but they did not correspond to the truth.

Nevertheless, climate increasingly played a role in the public discourse on childcare and children's health. Regular visits to hill stations were deemed to be good for health.[76] Already Hull had appreciated the hills with these warm words:

The hill stations offer a convenient compromise or substitute for the change to Europe. They possess every climatic advantage that can be wished, and experience has proved beyond all doubt, that children who have passed the age of teething, do thrive remarkably well, and grow up as robust and as healthy (physically) as they would in England.[77]

The relevant manuals likewise raised the Europeans' awareness of the benefits of a proper distance between the European children and the servants' quarters which had presumably lower sanitary standards.[78] A lack of care during the preparation of food (especially water and milk) was identified as a major cause of illness and death. Quite often, it was stipulated, that it was just 'ignorance, prejudice, and carelessness' of the servants or the locals, which constituted hazards to the European children's health.[79] Even these brief hints render evidence for our assumption that the debate on children's health was deeply embedded in contemporary colonial or 'oriental' discourses.

But it was only with the onset of the twentieth century that we witness an increasing awareness about proper hygienic conditions as a precondition for children's health in the tropics. A number of printed manuals such as Kate Platt's *The Home and Health in India and the Tropical Colonies* from 1923 identified notably three preconditions to render a healthy environment to the children: hygienic surrounding, proper food and protection from tropical diseases (for example, by wearing mosquito-nets or a sun-shade).

PREPARING FOR DEATH AND FUNERAL

Because 'death was always our near companion' (Kipling), the Europeans always had to be prepared to die, and the most common way to secure the worldly estate was the creation of a will. Already from the seventeenth century, it was common even for ordinary sailors to draw up a will. Such wills from the English/British possessions have survived in large numbers at the India Office Records in London. From the onset of the eighteenth century, the Company authorities at Fort St. George tried to institutionalize the creation of wills by stipulating that all wills needed to be approved by the Company's Court at Madras. It was intended by such procedure to contain excessive donations (especially by Roman Catholics) to the church authorities as a compensation for administering will and estate. Notably, the transfer of funds to the possessions of the European competitors was to be avoided: '. . . complaints had reached the Governor and Council [of Fort St. George] that advantage was taken of this circumstance to convey a large portion of the effects of the deceased Roman Catholics to the Patriarch of Antioch at Pondicherry.'[80] However, this rule was not always observed.[81]

The will was usually written at a younger age. Jacob Eilbradt from the Dutch VOC, for instance, wrote his will in 1762 at the age of 20, when he was about to live for four more decades.[82] Nevertheless, nobody knew, when one would fall victim to a disease, accident or suicide. The bulk of the texts is composed in a standardized form which only leaves little space for individual deliberations on funeral and burial. Most begin like that of the ship commander Edward Todd from 1782: '. . . that is to say I recommend my soul to God that gave it and my body commit to the earth or sea which it shall please God to order.'[83] Another standardized phrase, which was quite common during the first half of the nineteenth century, was 'I . . . direct my body to be interred by my executors, in Christian burial ground, or, as circumstances will admit.'[84] The settlement of funeral charges was taken care of in many instances as in the case of Grove Gillis' will from 18 August 1780: 'In primis I will & desire that all my just debts and funeral charges be punctually & speedily discharged . . .'.[85] Do these lines bear witness to a distinct ethics or rather to distrust against the heirs?—It is a question, we cannot answer here.

Only in few instances, the British wills from the eighteenth and the first half of the nineteenth century render detailed information on the mode of burial and the creation of tomb monuments. Instead, they are largely confined to quite general statements even in this respect. According to the wills, most Europeans aspired a 'decent burial'. This, for instance, applies for John Green in 1821, who wished 'to be decently interred, without pomp, but in the plainest and least expensive manner . . .' .[86] However, the visual appearance of the burial grounds leaves the impression, that even such notions might have been, at least to some degree, standard phrases, which did not prevent the heirs from erecting opulent monuments after the funeral. In other instances, it was probably a mere lack of funds which gave rise to such wishes.

Only in very few instances, the wills render evidence for the desire for a more elaborate and extravagant funeral. Such idea is expressed in the last will of Charles Danvers, Company servant and private merchant, who died in 1720:

> My corpse is to be carried from the Town Hall at 7 o'clock at night. I desire that all the free merchants of my acquaintance to attend me in their palankeens to the place of burial; and as many of the Company's servants as I have had any intimacy within my lifetime; that all that attend me may have scarves and hat-bands decent. I desire that Mr. Mai and the charity boys, may go before my corpse and sing a hymn; my corpse to be carried by six Englishmen or more if occasion; the minister and the rest of the gentlemen following. I desire the Honourable Governor that I may have as many great guns fired as I am years old, which is now almost twenty-one. . . . After my corpse is buried, which I desire may be done very handsomely, the remainder of my estate I desire may be laid out in rice, and be given to the poor at the burial place as long as it lasts.[87]

Nevertheless, a small number of wills expresses clear wishes regarding the location of someone's future burial place such as the desire of being buried next to a relative, for example, one's own brother, as was expressed by Joseph Peter de Mello (1818): '. . . my body I commit to the Earth to be interred in the Capuchin Church at Madras in the same Grave that the body of my late brother Thomas de Mello was buried.'[88]

Another favoured location was the family vault as in the case of the Madras Solicitor James Conram Jeremiah (1853): 'First, I desire to be decently and privately buried in my Family's Vault at St. Mary's Madras, without any Funeral pomp, and wit as little expense as possible.'[89] Especially Roman Catholics from Madras used to express their desire to be buried on Catholic burial grounds.[90] In some instances, such wishes were emphasized by the prospect of gracious donations to the respective church (a procedure which was not welcomed by the Council of Fort St. George). In 1783, John Brown, a Roman Catholic, puts down: 'I give and bequeath to the Romish Church at Madras the sum of two hundred Pagodas and to the priests residing in the said church and all other priests that may accompany my corps to the grave five pagodas each of them.'[91]—a desire, which seems to be strikingly different to the expressions of many Anglicans regarding a burial 'without pomp'.

Nevertheless, donations were similarly common among members of the Anglican, Reformed or Lutheran community, but they had a more 'social' appearance. In 1756, Jan Carsten Warner, lieutenant and equipagemeester in the service of the Dutch VOC not only endowed the Calvinist community at Nagapattinam with 200 pagodas, but also the Lutheran Mission at Tranquebar with a substantial amount.[92] Notably, the clerics themselves mention the transfer of their belongings, not just funds, but also material objects like books, to the church.[93]

After the death of a Company employee in English, Dutch, French or Danish service, the legal matters concerning his death were settled according to a more or less fixed schedule. First, the belongings of the deceased were sealed. After this, the last will was viewed to check the name of the executor of the deceased's estate. Finally, the council of the place officially handed over all affairs to the executor, namely the settling of debts and other demands from the estate.[94]

Very little is known about the funeral services in early colonial south India, especially of the Dutch, but there is no reason to believe that they were very different from the comparatively well-recorded funeral practices in Dutch Batavia. A funeral in Batavia followed a distinct procedure. Those of wealthy individuals tended to be conspicuously lavish, giving rise as early as 1658 to the issuing of a placard (*plakkaat*) by the Company authorities prohibiting the display of excessive luxury (*weelde*) during funerals. This measure, however, achieved the opposite of its aim, since the penalty for violation—payment of a fine (*boete*)—only added an inconspicuous but perfectly apparent expenditure to the open display of luxury at a funeral.[95] The funeral procession mirrored the social hierarchy and was thus subject to competition among the mourners for a place up front, indicating social prominence. Quarrels on order and precedence were sufficiently frequent to bring the VOC in 1718 to impose a protocol on Company officials at funerals. Not until 1753 was a general funeral regulation issued.[96]

Immediately after death in a Dutch settlement, the body of the deceased was cleaned, dressed and laid in an open coffin. A guard comprising friends or relatives of the deceased formed a night watch.

Letters announcing the death and the forthcoming funeral service (*doodbriefjes*) were printed and circulated by so-called *bidders*. The higher the social standing of the deceased, the larger the format of the *doodbriefje*. The funeral service itself started with a procession from the house of the deceased to the church or burial ground; at the head was the coffin and its bearers, followed by the *bidders* and the remaining mourners. In some instances an image eulogizing the deceased or displaying his coat of arms was carried in front of the procession. From 1743 onwards, at least in Batavia, it was compulsory to employ professional pallbearers from the garrison. It was not unknown for the corpses of members of the ruling elite to be carried on horse carriages. The service itself, which usually took place in the late afternoon and was illuminated by torches or candles, was followed by a reception that tended toward opulence. The only obviously democratic feature of the event was that all the guests, irrespective of rank, would smoke their pipes together in front of the house of the deceased.[97]

Most of the wills stipulate the financing of the funeral of its author, which gives rise to the assumption that funeral expenses might have been substantial and worth being mentioned in the will. The accounts of the Zion Church from Danish Tranquebar shown in Table 6 render an excellent insight into the fact that funerals constituted a substantial source of income, while baptisms or weddings were much less frequent and generally yielded smaller amounts.

The figures clearly show that the church incomes gained from funeral services far exceeded the income from baptisms or weddings. The average annual income was not constant, but even in

TABLE 6: FEES CHARGED AT ZION CHURCH, TRANQUEBAR

(Average p.a. in Rd. Tranq. Cour.)[98]

Period	Baptisms	Weedings	Funerals
August 1781–July 1785	9.3	7.8	97.0
August 1789–July 1793	13.3	6.3	37.1
August 1800–July 1804	10.0	12.0	56.8
August 1809–July 1813	7.9	5.9	43.7

'bad' years, as between 1789 and 1793, it was twice as much as the income gained from baptisms and weddings put together.

How much money was spent for an individual funeral at Tranquebar can be gleaned from the data which show that the average expenses for a single funeral of adults significantly increased between the 1780s and 1812, whereas the average amount for children's funerals became less within the same period (Table 7). What made funerals more expensive for adults during this period? The fee for the grave charged by the church did not increase during the entire period under review and always remained Rd. 4.00. The expenses for bell-ringing remained identical at Rd. 3.17 as well.[99] Instead, people spent more money for outfit and decoration of funerals after 1800. A frequently used 'Liig-Tæppet' (pall) cost around Rd. 0.3 during the 1780s, whereas an opulent 'Liig-klæde' to cover the corpse of the deceased was sold at Rd. 2.3 after 1800. A few bodies still received the cheaper version of the linen for Rd. 1.3. Several items only came into use at the end of the eighteenth century, such as the expensive so-called 'Liig Geridongs', stands or tables (gueridons) for laying the body, or candles and organ.[100] This more luxurious outfitting of the burial functions has to be seen in the context of the larger and more elaborate sepulchral monuments which appeared in the cemeteries during the same period. However, poorer members of the colonial communities, who enjoyed a more modest funeral, were usually freed from charges.[101] This notably applies to members of the colonial elite, who became poor at a higher age such as Henrik Olivarius, a former customs officer from Tranquebar.

TABLE 7: AVERAGE EXPENSES FOR A FUNERAL AT ZION CHURCH

(in Rd. Tranq. Cour.)[102]

Period	Adults	Children
August 1781–July 1785	6.34	3.84
August 1800–July 1804	7.34	2.50
August 1808–July 1812	8.95	2.44

Social distinction played a decisive role even after death in colonial south India which transpires from the British sources as well. Around 1800, the Madras Vestry divided funerals into two classes (which also might have been the case in the other European settlements): 'In burials, the rule shall be governed by this distinction: Those who use the best pall (Europe black cloth) shall be considered in the first class, those who do not use the best pall shall be allotted to the second class.'[103] While most poor Europeans did not enjoy a special ceremony at all,[104] the members of the social elite were in most instances commemorated by a comprehensive funeral service. A funeral sermon eulogizing the character of the deceased next to the coffin inside the church usually constituted the centrepiece of the service honouring a member of the elite. When the surgeon and scientist Edward Bulkeley died in 1713, William Stevenson, chaplain of St. Mary's Church in Fort St. George, for instance, wrote a sermon as one of his first tasks after having occupied this new position.[105]

The funeral sermon was in many instances not only created for being presented at the funeral itself, but it rendered a perfect commemoration of the deceased later in print. However, it is extremely difficult to identify printed funeral sermons from colonial India except in a very few outstanding cases. For instance, when Governor-General Cornwallis died in far distant Calcutta in 1805, Dr. Kew, the Chaplain at Fort St. George, held a funeral sermon, which was ordered to be printed by the government 'at the public expense; and that when printed a sufficient number of copies be circulated to the principal military stations under this Presidency'.[106] Next to the sermon, a special illumination featured the funeral service of the well-to-dos.[107] Also the ringing of church-bells in the course of the service, expressed a higher social rank.[108]

The funeral service commemorating a deceased of the highest social rank usually proved to emerge as a social event. In October 1791, Lt. Col. Moorhouse, who had been killed during the war against Tipu Sultan's troops at Bangalore, was honoured with an opulent burial service, which was carried out at the expense of the East India Company. After the Military Board at Fort St. George had received the information, that his corpse had been dispatched from Bangalore to Madras, a committee was established to arrange the funeral.[109] The body was carried all the way from Bangalore to Madras, which took about half a year. Afterwards, it was temporarily laid out inside the Grand Lodge of the Freemasons. From here, it was brought by a large procession along the burial ground to St. Mary's Church. The procession was headed by the Governor, the members of the Grand Lodge, six pallbearers and three chaplains, who wore silk scarves and hat bands. The military funeral party consisted of thirteen officers and 300 soldiers, including a firing-party firing salutes on the way. Finally, a funeral oration was held, before the body was interred inside the church.[110]

Military honours like firing gun salutes or marching soldiers contributed a sense of grandeur to a funeral. In July 1746, a captain of a French naval vessel died off Pondicherry. The subsequent procedures are described by the Dubash Ananda Ranga Pillai thus:

> The captain of one of the five sail which recently arrived, and whose name is not known to me, died this morning, after an illness. The colours of his ship were half-masted, and minute guns were fired until his remains were interred, when a salvo was discharged by the whole fleet together. The funeral took place at half-past 5 this evening.

Ananda Ranga Pillai reports on the funeral itself as well:

> Same day, the funeral of the naval captain who died this morning took place in the evening. Two hundred soldiers formed the procession, which marched with the royal standard, and with drums and pipes. M. de la Bourdonnais and all the captains of the ship accompanied it, and were present at the interment of the corpse in the church. The ceremony was performed in an imposing manner; the soldiers fired three volleys, and each ship twenty-one guns: seven were also fired from the fort.[111]

Ananda Ranga Pillai's observations leave no doubt about the fact that the funeral service not only served as a commemoration of the deceased captain, but that it simultaneously put on show the claim for imperial power and contributed to the emergence of colonial power-discourses in the 'Orient'.

While the discrete interment of adherents of denominations other than the official Anglican one was tolerated by the English company authorities in south India, the public display of supposedly unconform rites and processions during the funeral was heavily contested. Especially the first decades of the history of Fort St. George were characterized by the activities of French Roman Catholic priests, who obviously were tolerated if not supported by individual members of the Council. Complaints were raised in 1658 that 'First they are allowed at the burial of their dead to move before the corpse with bell, book, candle and cross, to the great discontent of those that know not how to remedy it. . . .'[112] However, it seems the Company authorities had no means of opposing this practice, since a comparative large number of Catholics and their families lived at Fort St. George.

The death of a wealthier or of a higher-ranking Christian Indian was similarly followed by a prescribed procedure. After the death had become known to the local authorities, it was ordered to seal the house and other properties of the deceased. If needed, the estate of the person was guarded by peons or by members of the local court to prevent plunder. The body was properly dressed and put into a coffin. Depending on the reputation or the social status of the deceased, a longer or shorter procession accompanied the corpse to the church—either early in the morning or during the evening hours. After the final rites, the coffin was lowered into a vault or into the dug-out earth.[113]

Exhumation after a proper funeral did not significantly contribute to the shaping of the cemeteries and was mainly confined to a small number of deceased who had belonged to the European elites and whose descendants could afford exhuming the bones of the beloved and prestigiously sending them back to Europe. This, for example, applies to the bones of General Sir Eyre Coote, the hero of Wandiwash, who suffered a stroke when sailing from Calcutta to Madras in 1783. Only a few days after his arrival, he died at Fort St. George, despite the application of electricity as a quite modern means of medical treatment. His body was interred in St. Mary's Church only to be exhumed and returned to Europe nine months later.[114] Another example is General De Bussy, who died in Pondicherry in 1785 at the age of 67 while playing cards. His body was embalmed and laid to rest for a later transport to

Europe, but because of the outbreak of the French Revolution, his corpse was secretly shifted to an unknown place near the cathedral at Pondicherry and buried there as a means of protection in case of revolutionary turmoil.[115]

NOTES

1. IOR, N/2, Ecclesiastical Returns Madras. Landsarkivet for Sjælland, Lolland-Falster & Bornholm, Sogn Nr. 777, Tranquebar Zions Kirkebog, 1767–1845 (microfiche).
2. Woods, 'Infant Mortality in Britain', pp. 74f.
3. For example, the Directors of Fort St. George wrote by 12 December 1800 to the clergy of Madras: 'Having of late experienced much inconvenience by your not having furnished us from time to time with registers of births, marriages and burials, as well as those at the subordinate settlements as at your Presidency, we now direct that due care be taken in future to transmit to us annually in duplicate correct registers of all births, marriages, and burials at your Presidency, and from all your subordinate settlements properly attested'. Quoted from Penny, *Church in Madras*, vol. 1, p. 406.
4. Woods, 'Infant Mortality in Britain', p. 74.
5. The enormous amount of data did not allow the recording of all entries of the first half of the nineteenth century. A representative sample of six years was thus chosen.
6. Shorters, *A Wasting Historical Asset?*
7. Ibid., p. 8.
8. Regarding this problem in general see Bassi, Introduction, pp. 2f.
9. Data gained from the first St. Mary's Cemetery (Guava Garden) and the present St. Mary's Cemetery. The monuments of the former burial ground are to be found around St. Mary's Church today.
10. Shorters, *A Wasting Historical Asset?*, p. 12.
11. Arnold, *Colonizing the Body*. Arnold perceives colonial medicine as an eminent means of exerting colonial power in India; see, for instance, p. 8: 'In part, therefore, the history of colonial medicine, and of the epidemic diseases with which it was so closely entwined, serves to illustrate the more general nature of colonial power and knowledge and to illuminate its hegemonic as well as its coercive processes'.
12. Arnold, *Colonizing the Body*, p. 11.
13. Ibid.

14. Ibid., p. 24.
15. Gründler, Malabarischer Medicus, manuscript, 1711, (Archive of the Francken's Foundation, Halle).
16. Arnold, *Colonizing the Body*, p. 23.
17. Ibid., p. 159.
18. Hull, *Anglo-Indian's Vade-Mecum*, pp. 253–309.
19. Ibid., p. 265.
20. Ibid., p. 266.
21. Ibid., pp. 265f.
22. Ibid., p. 259.
23. Quoted after: Arnold, *Colonizing the Body*, pp. 160f.
24. Malden, *List of Burials at Madras*.
25. Arnold, *Colonizing the Body*, see notably Figure 2 on p. 165.
26. Wilkinson, *Two Monsoons*, p. 25.
27. Hull, *Anglo-Indian's Vade-Mecum*, p. 260.
28. Dickens (ed.), *All The Year Round* , p. 104.
29. Ibid., pp. 104f.
30. Arnold, *Colonizing the Body*, p. 165.
31. Love, *Vestiges of Old Madras*, vol. 3, pp. 557f.
32. Malden, *List of Burials*.
33. Labouvie, *Andere Umstände*, p. 168.
34. Malden, *List of Burials*.
35. *Diary of Ananda Ranga Pillai*, vol. 1, p. 259.
36. Wilkinson, *Two Monsoons*, p. 194.
37. Penny, *Church in Madras*, vol. 1, p. 598. Wilkinson, *Two Monsoons*, pp. 34f.
38. IOR, N/2/32, 11 November 1853.
39. See, for example, Corporal Damant of Danish Tranquebar, who 'hængte sig selv' (hung himself) in October 1796. Zions Kirkebog, 15 October 1796. IOR, G/26/12, *Diary of William Puckle*, September 1675, p. 42.
40. Zions Kirkebog, 11 December 1798 and 17 December 1798.
41. IOR, G/26/12, Diary of William Puckle, 9 October 1675: 'That it was Dilirium y[t] took him [Mr. Cholmsly] in his sickness having fancied for three days that he was dying & thereupon tempted to make a short work'.
42. IOR, N/2/18-19, Funerals 1835, 1 November 1835.
43. Ibid., 29 October 1835 (Henry Greswell).
44. Wilkinson, *Two Monsoons*, p. 201.
45. IOR, P/333/4, letter from the Rev. Geo. Knox to the Venerable Archdeacon of Madras, 19 February 1848.
46. See, for instance, *Diary of Ananda Ranga Pillai*, vol. 1, p. 176, 7 August 1741.

47. *Diary of Ananda Ranga Pillai*, pp. 100f.
48. See for example, Woods, *Infant Mortality in Britain*; Perrenoud, *Child Mortality in Francophone Europe*, pp. 28f.
49. Dyson, *Infant and Child Mortality in the Indian Subcontinent*, p. 113.
50. Thomlinson, *Population Dynamics*, p. 99.
51. IOR, N/2/1, Ecclesiastical Returns Madras. No births were recorded for the years 1744, 1747–9, 1750, 1761, 1764 and 1767, or the data were not legible respectively.
52. Investigated years: 1825–6, 1835–6, 1845–6.
53. Zions Kirkebog, 1767–1845.
54. *Diary of Ananda Ranga Pillai*, vol. 1, p. 201, 10 October 1742.
55. Labouvie, *Andere Umstände*, pp. 166–7.
56. Woods, *Infant Mortality in Britain*, p. 84.
57. Buettner, p. 48.
58. Woods, *Infant Mortality in Britain*, p. 75.
59. Source: IOR, N/2/1, Ecclesiastical Returns Madras. No dates of birth were recorded for the years 1739, 1744, 1747–9, or the data were not legible respectively.
60. Zions Kirkebog, 1767–1845.
61. See for example, Zions Kirkebog, 1767–1845, 12 August 1838: 'Blev paa den gamle Kirkegaard begraved uden Jordspaakastelse Mr. Th. Heals og Hustrues Marg. Heals dødfødte Dren-gebarn'. The Roman-Catholic concept of 'limbo'—the place, where unbaptized babies went—was officially only declined by Pope Benedict XVI in 2007; see: *The Hindu*, 22 April 2007, p. 20.
62. Ibid., 10 September 1801.
63. Ibid., 8 July 1802, 31 January 1805.
64. Data recorded in the baptism files dating prior to 1770 are incomplete or illegible for the years 1744, 1750, 1761, 1764 and 1767.
65. Woods, *Infant Mortality in Britain*, p. 76.
66. Malden, *List of Burials*.
67. Love, *Vestiges of Old Madras*, vol. 3, p. 558.
68. Grove/Chappell, *El Niño*, p. 9.
69. Archiv der Franckeschen Stiftungen Halle (AFSt), M 2 B : 2, J.E. Geister, *Wind und Wetter Beobachtungen, 1732–1737*. See likewise Glaser/Militzer/Walsh, *Weather and Climate at Madras*.
70. Glaser/Militzer/Walsh, *Weather and Climate at Madras*, p. 79.
71. Quoted from the translation into English by Glaser/Militzer/Walsh, *Weather and Climate at Madras*, p. 62.
72. Grove/Chappell, *El Niño*, p. 9.

73. Love, *Vestiges of Old Madras*, vol. 3, p. 558.
74. Glaser/Militzer/Walsh, *Weather and Climate* at Madras.
75. Hull, *Anglo-Indian's Vade-Mecum*, p. 325.
76. Buettner, *Empire Families*, p. 33.
77. Hull, *Anglo-Indian's Vade-Mecum*, p. 346.
78. Platt, *The Home and Health in India and the Tropical Colonies*.
79. Quoted after Buettner, *Empire Families*, p. 33.
80. Quoted after Talboys Wheeler, *Madras in the Olden Time*, p. 244.
81. Ibid.
82. Peters, *In steen geschreven*, p. 186.
83. IOR L/AG/34/29/186, Edward Todd, 1782.
84. IOR L/AG/34/29/222, George Boyd, 10 November 1818.
85. IOR L/AG/34/29/186, Grove Gillis, 18 August 1780.
86. IOR L/AG/34/29/222, Madras Wills 1822/23, John Green, 16 April 1821. Also: ibid., Antonio Pereira, 22 May 1822.
87. Quoted after Wilkinson, *Two Monsoons*, p. 168.
88. IOR L/AG/34/29/222, Joseph Peter de Mello, 1818.
89. IOR, Madras Wills, Administrations & Inventories, September 1801 to December 1802, James Conram Jeremiah, 3 October 1853.
90. In 1816, Edward Lewcock desired to be buried 'within the Roman Catholic Church in the Black Town of Madras'. IOR L/AG/34/29/222, Edward Lewcock, 6 May 1816.
91. IOR L/AG/34/29/186, John Brown, 13 February 1783.
92. Peters, *In steen geschreven*, p. 192.
93. See, for example Consultations, 30 October 1696, on the Chaplain of St. Mary's Church, Fort St. George, Richard Elliott, in: Penny, *Church in Madras*, vol. 1, p. 116: '. . . he hath left his books to the Library and 250 pagodas to the Church.'
94. See, for example, Streynsham Master's report on the death of Thomas Whitehead, Chaplain of the English factory at Masulipatnam, in: Penny, *Church in Madras*, vol. 1, pp. 62f.
95. *Oud Batavia*, p. 156.
96. Ibid., p. 157.
97. Ibid., pp. 158–61.
98. Compiled from Zions Kirkes Regnskaber. The Rd. Tranq. Courant amounted to approximately 18 per cent less than the Danish Rd.
99. In the sources: Rd. 3 and fanam 2.
100. See for example the funerals of Mrs. Rehling (29 January 1809) and Mrs. Lindgreen (31 January 1812).
101. See, for example, Zions Kirkebog, Tranquebar, 30 January 1800: 'Gl. Kg.

Døde Aron Lindenboom paa Hospitalet of blev begravet paa den gamle Kirkegaard. Han var Styrman og en Svendsker af Fødsel. Fik fri Grav og Liigklæde uden Betaling, da han døde i meget fattige Omstændigheder.' Ibid., 29 December 1800: 'Gl. Kg. Hr. Tolder Hendrik Olivarius begravet paa den gamle Kirkegaard. Klokkerne ringede og det nyere Liigklæde, Bænk og Skamle brugte. Omkostningerne Enken eftergivet formedelst hendes fattige Omstændigheder'.

102. Zions Kirkes Regnskober.

103. Quoted after Wilkinson, *Two Monsoons*, p. 15.

104. See, for example, Zions Kirkebog, Tranquebar, 28 October 1786: '. . . Regiment Feldskiær Bøtticher uden nogen ceremonie'.

105. Penny, *Church in Madras*, vol. 1, p. 144.

106. See ibid., p. 451.

107. See, for example, the funeral of Adolf Fridrich Restorff at the Zion Church of Tranquebar on 15 August 1786: '. . . blev liig tale holden og kirken illumineret.' Zions Kirkebog, 15 August 1786.

108. See, for example, Zions Kirkebog, Tranquebar, 17 January 1787; see also: Zions Kirkebog, 3 September 1832: 'Blev paa den nye kirkegaard begravet dend 2 Septbr. Klokker ved Zions Kirke og Skolelærer ved Zions Skole Jens Jacob Wodschow – født paa Sønderskov ved Ribe i Jylland den 8de Martii 1773. Han har været her i Tranquebar i 33 Aar, og forestaaet sit Embede, som Klokker og Skolelærer omt. 32 Aar. Liget blev nedsat i Kirken, medens Liigtalen holdtes, før og efter Talen blev afsjunget 2de Sunge, der saavel som Talen tolkede den Afdøden store Værd som Menneske og Lærer. Derefter blev Liget udført og nedsat i graven, hvor Jord paakastede.'

109. Military Consultations, 29 October 1791, see Penny, *Church in Madras*, vol. 1, p. 397.

110. Garrison Orders, 31 October 1791; Military Consultations, 3 January 1792; Letters Home, 16 January 1792, 130, 131, Mil.; see: Penny, *Church in Madras*, vol. 1, pp. 396ff.

111. *Diary of Ananda Ranga Pillai*, vol. 2, p. 128.

112. See Penny, *Church in Madras*, vol. 1, p. 27.

113. See, for example, the description of the death and funeral of Kanakarayar Murali, the chief Dubash of Pondicherry, in *Diary of Ananda Ranga Pillai*, vol. 1, pp. 310–13 (12–13 February 1746).

114. Wilkinson, *Two Monsoons*, p. 42.

115. Ibid., p. 130.

CHAPTER 2

The Cemeteries

PRESERVATION AND DECAY

Cemeteries have always been subject to changes in extent, structure and in the number of monuments.[1] Walls and gates have been altered and new monuments erected, whereas others have crumbled over time. The dead were interred, while a smaller number were exhumed to be buried elsewhere. When investigating burial grounds of the past, we must set aside our current perception of cemeteries as places of eternal peace and rest with manicured lawns and hedges. They were often inhabited and even desecrated by the residents, hawkers and animals, which lead to their destruction, sometimes long before they were permanently closed. Similarly, the Indian climate with its monsoonal rainfalls and the demand for land amongst the population, along with scarcity of funds, had a devastating impact on the monuments in the long run. The reasons for such decay before, and even more so after Independence, shed a revealing light on people's self-perception and political priorities.

It has been contended in a very recent study, that the decay of colonial cemeteries in South Asia was merely a result of a distinct post-colonial perception of the colonial past.[2] Cemeteries are thought to symbolize not just personal mourning but also imperial aspirations, which puts them in an ambivalent and precarious position in today's India. These considerations cannot be denied, and there can be no doubt that the protection of monuments was regarded as a patriotic task within the British Raj as well. In 1840, G. Trevor, the Chaplain at Bangalore, wrote to the Bishop of Madras about the condition of a number of British soldiers' graves, dating from the end of the eighteenth century, located around the Haider

Ali and Tipu Sultan monuments at Seringapatnam, '. . . it [i.e. the burial ground] is now so completely abandoned that the natives are growing vegetables among the grave stones which still retain their inscriptions to the memory of the dead. The feelings of religion no less than of patriotism are wounded by such a neglect of the remains of our countrymen. . . .'[3] This appeal to the authorities' patriotism indicates an acute awareness of the connection between colonial dignity and tomb monuments, and proved to be most effective. The Lord Bishop of Madras immediately took the matter further and underlined in a letter to the Governor at Madras: 'The expediency and desirability of honouring the remains of our gallant countrymen are too apparent. . . .'[4] Soon after, the British resident at Mysore was entitled 'to adopt such measures as you may deem fit for rescuing the graves alluded to from desecration'.[5] The tendency to link the glory of imperial military success with the monuments is apparent in many other places, including in a number of inscriptions.[6]

However, the postulation of a dichotomy between commemoration of the dead as a distinct element of the self-perception of the British Raj and post-colonial neglect proves to be too short-sighted. This is evident from the fact that many colonial cemeteries were already in a severe state of decay even during the colonial period. Even before Independence, travellers and Company representatives frequently deplored either the poor quality of the English stone slabs or deliberate neglect of the cemeteries.[7] Furthermore, it was the British themselves who deliberately reduced financial aid and abandoned many cemeteries after Independence. After 1947, a number of consecrated cemeteries were actually cared for by the Indian Christian communities instead. A reader's letter to *The Times* of 1949 clearly reveals a sense of give and take: 'The British restored to dignity and maintained in decency the memorials of Hindu, Buddhist, and Muslim. Is it too much to hope that their successors will do the same for British Monuments? The friendly and kindly Indian people will surely do their part.'[6]

Although written material on the maintenance of cemeteries prior to the nineteenth century is very limited, and offers merely a rough glimpse of the situation, decay had already set in during

Early Modern times. Major evidence is restricted to St. Mary's Cemetery near Fort St. George in Madras—known in contemporary records as the 'Guava Garden'. The burial ground itself was owned by the East India Company, and it seems the Company representatives did not take much care of it despite the protests of the local clergy. At the onset of the eighteenth century (or probably even earlier), toddy trees had been planted here, whose produce was regularly sold, contributing to the income of the local government. If such commerce might have been tolerable, the grazing of buffaloes, the erection of stables and the sale of toddy on the ground seems to have been inacceptable. In 1710, the clergymen wrote a letter of complaint to the Council:

> That whereas the monuments of the dead, and the ground where they are interred are held by most people in some measure sacred, and not lightly applied to any common or profane use, yet it is our misfortune that the English burying place in Fort St. George (where so many of our relations friends and acquaintances lie buried) is not only not kept in that decent and due manner it ought to be, but every day profaned and applied to the most vile and indecent uses. (. . .) The Toddy men have people employed there all the day, and almost all the night, in drawing and selling of Toddy. (. . .) And then about eight o'clock at night after work is done, it is such a resort of basket makers, scavengers, people that look after buffaloes, and other Pariahs, to drink Toddy, that all the punch houses in Madras have not half the revise in them.[9]

The clerics blamed the local people and animals for desecrating the cemetery with the silent tolerance of the government, which doubtless derived profit from the situation. A dichotomy is visible here not between the Indians and the Europeans as one might expect, but between faith, morality and tradition on one side and commerce on the other. The local ministers initiated an attempt to construct a corporate identity by promoting an image of patriotism, since they deliberately speak of the English burial place and refer to friends and relatives being buried there. In this instance, the cemetery emerges as a platform to mirror common sense and social virtues against the temptations of the material world. The topoi visualized in this discourse can be found in many other discourses on morality and the virtues of the Early Enlightenment in England.[10]

The ministers' appeal was only a partial success, because whilst the local government had the scavengers and Company buffaloes removed, no attempt was made to get rid of the toddy consumers.[11] Six years later a decision of purely pragmatic nature assisted the cause, when a house belonging to the Church was pulled down to make space for the erection of a new hospital. After brief negotiations, the authorities decided to transfer ownership of the toddy trees in the Guava Garden from the East India Company to St. Mary's Church, in addition to providing financial compensation:

> That the old toddy trees in the burial place, commonly called the Guava Garden, which are very much decayed, and bring in no more at present than 20 pagodas per annum be given and granted to the Church for ever; and that the sum of 300 pagodas be paid to them out of cash in full of all demands for the house afore mentioned.[12]

It is not reported, if the ground was actually cleared afterwards. But as the records of that time keep silent on this matter, it is likely that the church ousted the toddy drinkers soon after. Nevertheless, the case of St. Mary's Cemetery would not have been unusual in the Western world. Such behaviour was obviously quite common in late Medieval and Early Modern cemeteries in Europe, as many complaints came about commerce, dance, gambling or theatre show there.[13]

The second half of the eighteenth century proved detrimental to burial grounds due to the impact of the frequent wars fought amongst the Europeans and against the Indian powers. Two major encounters have left clear traces in south India: the long-running conflicts between the British and the French and the wars between the British and Mysore, which made the British emerge as the leading power in the south before 1800. Great Britain and France were at war in India for about two decades between 1744 and 1763, without the interruption of seven years enjoyed in Europe after the Peace of Aix-la-Chapelle. It was not until the 1790s that the conflict was finally decided in favour of the British, when Tipu was soundly defeated at the battle of Seringapatnam.[14]

It was St. Mary's Cemetery which was more affected by the wars than any other burial ground. During the French siege of Fort St. George in 1758–9, the French utilized the walls of the Guava Garden as a means of shelter from the British canons, and from behind which to fire onto the Fort. After the end of this siege and the withdrawal of the French in March 1759, the Council of Fort St. George eliminated this danger by levelling the cemetery walls and by demolishing the brick monuments. Only three monuments commemorating members of the most prominent Madras families—the Yale, Hymners, Powney, Heron, Goodwin, Proby and Lucas—remain in their original position near today's Law College (Plates 2 and 3). Most stone slabs were removed and rearranged around St. Mary's Church within the Fort.

During the wars against Haider Ali and Tipu Sultan, the slabs, also those lying *in situ* inside the church, were deemed suitable platforms for the guns on the ramparts of Fort St. George. Here they remained for 25 years from 1782 until 1807, when they were returned (with the exception of the memorials from inside the church) by the Military Board.[15] An increasing consciousness of the antiquity of the slabs may have contributed to their return from the ramparts despite the fact that the Napoleonic wars were not yet over.[16] We will probably never know the true extent of war damage to St. Mary's Cemetery: not only were many stone-slabs or epitaphs destroyed, but it should be remembered that many of these would have originally been affixed to larger monuments made of brick, as described by the English traveller Lockyer during his visit to Madras in 1711.

By 1805, all British ecclesiastic premises and properties in south India had been placed under the authority of the government at Fort St. George, and the vestries of the individual churches withdrawn. The Public and Military Works Departments were henceforth responsible for the maintenance of the cemeteries in the British possessions.[17]

It seems that this administrative reform generated a certain degree of professionalism and efficiency in the future management of the European cemeteries in British India. Their maintenance now became an issue within a well-organized colonial administration. Local church bodies or Company servants such as collectors could now refer the deplorable state of affairs in the burial grounds directly to the government in Fort St. George, which either took decisions itself or delegated the matter to the relevant departments or other institutions. Most—even smaller—cemeteries were now encircled by brick walls, which replaced the hedges used hitherto.[18] Even on the periphery of the colonial territories, cemeteries were put into better shape after 1805, as in the case of the burial ground at Palamcottah which was renovated and later eulogized for its well-kept monuments by the Danish Missionary David Rosen.[19] Nevertheless, the maintenance of architectural features had to be complemented by proper gardening, which does not always seem to have been the case even after 1805. Based on his observations during the first few decades of the nineteenth century, the British soldier H. Beavan compares Christian with Muslim burial sites:

> It is strange that so touching an example had not been followed by the European residents, who at a very small cost, might render the places of interment destined for their brethren, far less revolting than their present aspect. A few labourers attached to each cemetery would keep the whole in order; and as flowers spring up spontaneously in many places, little care or cultivation would be required to convert the coarse dark grass, which seems to afford a harbour for snakes and other venomous reptiles, into a blooming garden; and though, in consequence of the number of tombs, which are crowded, as in England, into the same enclosure, and their inferiority both in size, design and beauty of the material, a Christian cemetery never could be rendered so imposing and attractive as those spacious and carefully tended pleasure-grounds surrounding the mausoleum. . . .[20]

This comparison shows that the European cemetery was not chiefly perceived as an internal Christian matter but as a showcase for European culture in competition with Muslim culture. The way of tending the graves of deceased countrymen emerged as an indicator of civilization in the cultural encounter with the other.

At the same time, a number of cemeteries belonging to erstwhile rivals, such as the Dutch, the Portuguese and the Danes, were gradually integrated into this system during the first half of the nineteenth century. In a period of emerging European nationalism, cemeteries were regarded, even more so than before, as relics of a supposedly glorious colonial past, and after the Napoleonic wars their maintenance became subject to international treaties. For example, the conditions of Dutch withdrawal from Coromandel stipulated that their monuments be kept up by the British authorities.[21] Only then were long awaited repairs carried out in Dutch cemeteries such as Nagapattinam (Karikop) in 1832 and 1835.[22]

In the course of time, the condition of stone slabs in and around St. Mary's Church from the previous centuries deteriorated due to unknown reasons. Indeed, in many cases the only record of their existence can be found in the early anthologies of inscriptions from British India. This applies, for example, to Richard Elliott, one of the first chaplains of St. Mary's Church, who died in 1696. The only trace of the monument erected to him is the Latin inscription published in William Urquhart's *Oriental Obituary* in 1809.[23]

From the onset of the Early Enlightenment, opinions on the historical value of Early Modern tomb monuments were voiced in England. Thomas Addison famously raised this issue as early as 1711 in his article 'Reflections in Westminster Abbey'. However, in his opinion, it was the Dutch and not the English sepulchral monuments that deserved more attention: 'The Dutch, whom we are apt to despise for want of genius, show an infinitely greater taste of antiquity and politeness in their buildings and works of this nature, than what we meet with in those of our own country'.[24]

Throughout the eighteenth and nineteenth centuries though, the matter of antiquity hardly played any role in British India when decisions were made about funds for maintaining cemeteries. It was chiefly the fact that a cemetery was still in use, which secured funding, irrespective of nationality or religion, the historical value of monuments was not properly considered in such decisions. The case of the Dutch Buitenkerkhof in Pulicat exemplifies this. As early as 1794, large sections of the cemetery walls had collapsed, but the distractions of the Napoleonic wars prevented their repair. When the Principal Collector of North Arcot, Lord Ogilvie, visited Pulicat still in 1840, he did not deem it necessary to protect the seventeenth-century monuments. He notes: 'In the whole enclosure I can only count eleven slabs lying scattered in different parts with scarcely a vestige of masonry attached to them.

. . . it is not very probable that the old overturned tomb stones that have remained in that position for the last two hundred years, can be longer preserved. . . .'[25] The British authorities also proved to be rather parsimonious. Faced with the need to maintain two other old Dutch cemeteries in Pulicat in addition to the Buitenkerkhof, it was suggested that a hedge be planted around the burial ground instead of re-erecting a wall.[26]

Only at the end of the nineteenth century, did an increasing awareness of the historical significance of the monuments arise among the public and especially within the Archaeological Survey of India (ASI), which had been founded in 1861. This growing interest is not just reflected in an increasing number of anthologies of inscriptions from Indian cemeteries, as discussed in the introduction to the present volume, but even more in the fact that it now emerged as an issue for the ASI itself. One volume of the *New Imperial Series*, published by the ASI, is devoted to the *Monumental Remains of the Dutch East India Company in the Presidency of Madras*.[27] This is a clear indicator of the fact that the European (tomb) monuments now constituted part—albeit a minor one—of the archaeological and historical endeavours of the ASI. Whilst the proliferation of publications signals the growing appreciation of the historical worth of cemeteries, physical efforts of preserving outstanding monuments in single instances are more important. In the late nineteenth century, for example, 29 Portuguese and 19 Dutch stone slabs were removed from the floor of St. Francis' Church in Cochin and fixed along the walls to protect the fading inscriptions.[28] An investigation of the church shows that all the slabs have survived to the present day, but some have become even more illegible when the inscriptions are compared with the entries in Cotton's *List of Inscriptions*.[29]

The tradition of protecting outstanding monuments and burial grounds was taken up again by the ASI after Independence. Today, a number of European burial places and churches with interments is protected and maintained by the ASI. In this respect, this highly regarded institution is by no means affected by post-colonial indifference towards colonial cemeteries.[30]

The improved maintenance and increased awareness of the historical value of cemeteries in the course of the nineteenth century belie the fact that for financial reasons the British government was already pursuing a policy of transferring responsibility for the maintenance of British cemeteries abroad to foreign authorities from the end of the nineteenth century. As early as 1890, the government in London decided to hand over as many civil British cemeteries in foreign countries as possible to local church bodies, and so to withdraw financial support.[31] The expenses for military cemeteries were to be reduced as much as possible. Even if this policy applied to burial grounds in foreign countries, rather than in the colonies, it paved the way for future policy towards an independent India half a century later. Indeed, the relevant circular issued by the Foreign Office by March 1890 even constituted the basis of the deliberations of the British government, and especially of the Commonwealth Relations Office, in Downing Street, London during the process of the Transfer of Power.[32]

From the beginning of 1947, the British colonial authorities discussed the future of the European cemeteries in an independent India. The major institutions dealing with this issue were the (still British) Government of India Defence Department, the Metropolitan of the Church of India, Burma and Ceylon and representatives of the only recently established Office of the High Commissioner in New Delhi. In a decisive session on 25 February 1947, the principles of future maintenance were settled. It was contended, that 'the High Commissioner should assume overall responsibility for cemeteries and that under him should be two agencies for their maintenance', namely, the Indian office of the Imperial War Graves Commission responsible for military graves and a new agency in charge of civilian graves under the head of the British High Commission. The latter was to emerge soon after as the 'British Monuments and Graves Section Office of the High Commissioner for the United Kingdom New Delhi'.[33] The British Parliament subsequently granted funds for cemeteries in current use, scheduled for a decade, and the prospect of limited funds even for closed cemeteries was held out.[34]

In 1948, the ownership of the formerly British cemeteries possessed by the British-Indian government was shifted to the Indian government. Consecrated Christian cemeteries owned by the churches themselves—which comprised about half of the cemeteries—were handed over to the newly established Indian Church Trustees, which were subordinate to the Church of India, Pakistan, Burma and Ceylon.[35] The British High Commission in New Delhi was entrusted with administering the cemeteries belonging to the Indian government and considering their future fate. Cemetery Boards were founded in different parts of India. For south India, the South India Cemeteries Board was established.

Two principle sources of income were available for the maintenance of cemeteries and graves after Independence. These were fundings granted by the Indian and British governments respectively, as well as the interest from endowments originating from the pre-Independence period. During the first half of the 1940s, the cemeteries had received financial support from the Government of British India up to an amount of £45,000 annually, but the sum was significantly reduced after 1947.[36] The funds granted by the Indian government after Independence were much less again, since the cemeteries of the former colonial masters were, as might be expected, not on the priority list of Independent India. In 1951, the Indian government granted funds amounting to Rs. 20,000,[37] of which the South Indian Cemeteries Board received a sum of Rs. 5,553. In view of the enormous need for repairs, this 'extremely restricted'[38] sum proved to be too small to cause any significant effect and was soon eaten up by very basic repairs such as the reconstruction of walls, etc.[39]

The second source of income, the endowment funds, had been pooled in 1948. During the first half of the twentieth century they had constituted a major source of income for maintaining the cemeteries. Even if many of the relevant records seem to have perished, it is obvious that the interest accruing from the endowment capital rose significantly during that period. While, for example, the European cemetery of Kotagiri received Rs. 436 in the financial year 1925–6, an amount of Rs. 2,990 was transferred to Kotagiri in 1947–8.[40] From 1947, the capital of the funds annually yielded about 3 per cent, but the net income significantly deteriorated due to inflation and finally ceased during the 1960s.[41] It soon transpired that the interest from the endowment funds was sufficient only for maintenance of the endowed monuments alone.[42]

Another possible source—donations from the local church communities—proved to be limited. It is, for example, reported from Vijayawada that 'our handful of desperately poor Anglo–Indians cannot possibly meet the kind of major expenditure' facing the community.[43]

Apart from the British cemeteries, the problem arose as to how to handle the maintenance of the non-British European cemeteries in India from colonial times. On the occasion of discussions on the upkeep of about 80 graves of Polish refugees at Kolhapur from between 1939 and 1945, the British Foreign Office reduced the matter to a mere legal issue and came to the conclusion that 'no international convention applying to the upkeep of graves of foreign nationals' existed.[44] A policy of indifference and procrastination was also pursued towards the other former colonial powers in India. When the Portuguese ambassador in Delhi approached the British High Commission regarding the historical Portuguese graves in former British India, he was given lists of remaining monuments, but no further assistance was provided by the British.[45] The same applied to the Danish monuments in Tranquebar and Serampore near Calcutta. Brigadier H. Bullock of the British High Commission referred to 'some very interesting old Danish graves at Tranquebar' in a letter to the Commonwealth Relations Office from April 1949, inquiring, 'Do you think we might consider suggesting to the Danish Government that they should make some contribution towards the upkeep of these?'[46] The answer from Downing Street was as diplomatic as it was dilatory contending 'once the major questions of policy and organization have been cleared, to consider with the Foreign Office what should be done in regard to possible contributions from foreign Governments. . . . We will certainly bear in mind these Danish graves when doing so.'[47]

It was left chiefly to the Dutch to show a higher degree of interest in the fate of their monuments after Independence. The correspondence between the Dutch Embassy in New Delhi and the British High Commission reveals the Dutch willingness to sponsor the maintenance of Dutch monuments in Bengal, but not in south India. In 1953, the Dutch Embassy offered an annual grant for maintaining Dutch monuments in the cemetery of Berhampur in Bengal. Two years later, the money had still not been spent by the local church bodies, and no further grants are recorded.[48]

The most serious problem which remained was the maintenance of the cemetery walls, which tended to collapse, in many instances due to the impact of rains. The gaps created thereby would regularly tempt local people to allow their cattle to graze on the cemetery grounds, as is highlighted by the many complaints sent to the British High Commission.[49] Easy access to the cemeteries over dilapidated walls offered great opportunities for vandalism and theft. The demolition of 'the beautiful figure of an angel on my beloved daughter's grave' lamented by the Municipal Councillor of Kilpauk/ Madras was not an isolated incident.[50] It is further reported that 'there has been ruthless felling of trees at the Kilpauk and St. Mary's cemeteries in Madras. The former which is situated in a remote locality is so mercilessly ravaged, that it resulted in several tombstones and graves being damaged beyond repair.'[51] By 1956, about 300 trees had been cut illegally in Kilpauk Cemetery.[52] The funds that the South India Cemetery Board was able to offer on behalf of the British High Commission proved to be too meagre for any substantial repairs.[53]

Another common complaint in post-Independence India was the theft of iron from railings and fences erected around the graves. This was especially prevalent in the case of unprotected cemeteries such as the Nyegade Kirkegaard in Tranquebar, where theft of iron still occurred during the 1970s and after.[54] But even the Kilpauk Cemetery in Madras fell victim to the theft of iron:

> It is suffering at present from the depredation of thieves who have removed all available iron work from the monuments. . . . Such thieving is carried out during the hours of darkness, and owing to the size of the cemetery it is not possible for the caretaker to keep adequate watch during the night. Complaints have been repeatedly made to the police but they are unable to take effective action owing to the fact that a large portion (about 70 yards) of the surrounding wall has fallen, and this has given easy access to the most remote part of the cemetery.[55]

It is easy to identify where such thefts have occurred in the past for it usually leaves the kerbs surrounding the monuments with a number of empty holes, where formerly the railings were inserted.

After Independence, it was obvious that the large number (1,350) of formerly British or European cemeteries spread across entire India could not be fully maintained by the ever dwindling interest from the endowments and the meagre funding issued by the British Parliament and the Indian government. This problem was the subject of debate within the House of Lords as early as 1949. A statement by Lord Listowel gives a realistic picture of the future situation:

> Your Lordships will, I am sure, appreciate that a full-scale maintenance of all these cemeteries would be a formidable commitment, and I am bound quite frankly to admit that we shall not be able to continue to maintain some of the cemeteries on the old standard; indeed, there are certain cemeteries that we shall not be able to maintain to any extent. Nevertheless I hope to satisfy your Lordships that the Government are doing what they can to secure that, where cemeteries cannot be maintained their preservation will be safeguarded so far as local circumstances permit. In such cases our aim would be to secure that they should revert to nature in a dignified and decent manner.[56]

While the British High Commission granted funds for watchmen and repairs at a small number of burial grounds it regarded as 'show places',[57] it now proposed withdrawing support for a number of smaller unconsecrated cemeteries and handing full responsibility for them over to the Indian government. The consequences were described as thus: 'When a cemetery is formally abandoned, it automatically reverts to the Govt. of India for it is already in their property. Thereafter, the Govt. are entitled to do what they like with the land as it is understood that local Christians have no further use for it.'[58]

Critical voices[59] did not prevent the British government and the British High Commission in New Delhi from pursuing this policy once it had been agreed. In July 1954, Wallis Linnell, Chairman of the South India Cemeteries Board, submitted a list of 53 cemeteries recommended for abandonment. However, it very soon became obvious, that Linnell had made this list without the consent of the local church committees, possibly due to a lack of staff, and the issue had to be considered anew.[60] By October 1954, a memorandum by the British High Commission was able to put forward a list of nine cemeteries to be abandoned. In the end, a total of five lists, mainly comprising closed cemeteries that were not being maintained by a church or any other institution, or cemeteries that could no longer be traced, were compiled and handed over to the Indian government. These criteria unfortunately also applied to some ancient burial grounds containing several graves of historical importance. An eighteenth-century cemetery in Anjengo and the Old Dutch Cemetery at Cochin were thus returned to the Indian government by the first list. While the second memorandum, dated 26 November 1954, included 14 cemeteries of lesser historical significance, amongst the 10 cemeteries recommended for abandonment in the third list, dated 1 January 1955, were the seventeenth- and eighteenth-century Dutch cemeteries of Porto Novo and Palakollu. A further list of 11 burial grounds followed on 21 May 1960. This proposed the abandonment of the eighteenth-century burial ground of Rajahmundry and seven graves on Stonehouse Hill at Ootacamund—the oldest British graves in the Nilgiris.[61] Here a few tombs were still visible during the 1960s, but nothing remains now.[62] One of the six burial sites on the fifth list that followed in 1963 was the Nyegade Kirkegaard of Tranquebar.[63] Bearing in mind the words of Lord Listowel from 1949—'That the historically more important of the closed cemeteries shall be cared for in the same way',[64] i.e. with funding from the British High Commission—the lists clearly reveal the gradual decline in the commitment of the British government to the modest objectives it had set in the late 1940s.

Altogether, 46 cemeteries were handed over to the Indian government under the euphemistic phrase 'to allow them to revert to nature', the results of which can be seen today. Also the Government of India's assurance from 1949, 'that they will protect cemeteries from destruction and desecration in the same way as property belonging to the government themselves'[65] proved to be worthless in many cases. This can be seen from the fate of numerous burial places which were supposed to have 'reverted to nature'. The Stonehouse Hill Cemetery of Ootacamund containing the oldest European graves in the Nilgiris has entirely been cleared for the erection of new houses. And the European cemetery of Porto Novo with several remarkable Dutch graves, has become a dumping ground for waste and a public latrine (Plate 4).

The cemeteries under the care of the ASI have fared better. Notably Pulicat, with its seventeenth-century Dutch cemetery, has been put forward as a suitable destination for the developing heritage tourism industry (Plate 5). This site is situated close to today's Chennai/Madras and constitutes an ideal focus for short-term tourism. Preliminary studies have been carried out by the Indian National Trust for Art and Cultural Heritage, and the Royal Dutch Embassy has expressed its willingness to support such projects. However, the necessary infrastructure has still to be developed.[66] Today, Sadras is the site of advanced archaeological research. During the 1990s, the ASI restored the outer walls and the storehouses inside the fort. Archaeological excavations were carried out, which yielded an impressive number of Dutch artefacts such as Gouda smoking pipes and Delft blue pottery.[67]

TYPOLOGY AND SPATIAL DEVELOPMENT

The European cemeteries in India witnessed tremendous structural changes from the onset of the European enterprise in the East up to the twentieth century. However, it was not until the 1940s, when during the debates on the abandonment of British cemeteries in India typologies for a clear categorization were developed. At this time, it became common to differentiate between closed and open burial grounds, i.e. between cemeteries which were still in use at that time and those without current burials. Furthermore, a classification differentiating between churchyards, cemeteries, war graves notably of the First and Second World War and scattered monuments was developed.[68] A differentiation between open and closed grounds does not seem to be appropriate today, because almost all surviving European cemeteries have been closed in the meantime.[69] Also, the latter, formal differentiation neglects the historical perspective.

Investigating the burial ground in a historical perspective, another typology seems to be feasible. Broadly speaking, we can distinguish two periods of European expansion, which brought about distinct types of cemeteries: The first, which might be called the 'factory-period', is characterized by scattered European trading settlements along the shores of the Indian Ocean and further inland. During these times, the Europeans did not exercise military power which exceeded the immediate range of their possessions. Furthermore, they largely had to accommodate themselves to local traditions of communication and representation.

From the mid-eighteenth century, the Anglo–French Wars in India and especially the defeat of the Mughals in Bengal lead to a tremendous territorial expansion of the British East India Company. With the increase in European population complex family structures emerged in contrast to the individual merchants, who had carried out their businesses in the earlier period. Colonial metropolises such as Madras in the south or Calcutta and Bombay further north emerged, while Indo–European provincial towns grew in the hinterland. A special type of European settlement was the cantonment with chiefly military purposes and, from the 1820s, the hill stations in the mountains of the Eastern Ghats, Western Ghats or the Nilgiris.[70]

Against the backdrop of this structural change between the earlier and the latter period of European colonial expansion from about 1750 onwards, the following types may be considered:

- The 'Garden' during the factory period.
- The modern town cemetery in the age of territorial expansion.
- Burial grounds of hill stations.
- Cantonment cemeteries and war graves.
- The interment inside churches.
- Scattered monuments.

While the first category refers to the early period of European expansion in the subcontinent, the second to fourth represent the time of European territorial expansion. The last two types are to be found in both periods.

The remaining material evidence, however, poses a problem when applying any suitable typology: In several instances, it is not clear, if apparently undisturbed burial grounds actually accommodate ledgers *in situ* or if monuments have been transferred there at a later date. Such an assumption doubtlessly applies to the seventeenth- and early eighteenth-century ledgers in front of St. Mary's Church at Fort St. George or—outside our spatial range of observation—to St. John's Church in Calcutta.[71] At St. Mary's, a burial ground had never existed (in contrast to today's visual appearance), while the ledgers had been rearranged there from another place in the course of the Seven Years' War (Plate 6). Also, in other instances, doubts were raised such as in the case of the Dutch ledgers at Sadras.[72] Three places with Dutch monuments can be found at Sadras nowadays—two inside the fort and one about 200 m northwards near today's church. A well-maintained cemetery inside the fort, which is enclosed by a separate wall, contains 15 ledgers. During the field-studies carried out in 2004, two smaller stone slabs were found lying scattered on the ground inside the compound wall of the Dutch Fort close to the entrance gate—however, outside the enclosure accommodating the other ledgers. Some years before, those two monuments were obviously still placed on a burial ground north of the fortress.[73] This third plot outside the fortress compound displays merely ruined tombs without inscriptions. While only few vestiges of former monuments such as brick foundations survive on the latter site near the church today, Penny records a monument dating back to 1651, which was still to be met there at the beginning of the twentieth century.[74] It seems unlikely that several Dutch cemeteries were simultaneously in use at Sadras during the seventeenth century. We may presume instead, that the original burial ground with some likeliness was the latter one situated outside the fort, while the slabs commemorating the most distinguished deceased were later shifted inside for better protection.[75] This observation is supported by the fact, that the plot outside the fort still accommodates dilapidated brick constructions, while the plot inside the fortress does not: The subconstructions were obviously not shifted and left to their fate.

Another shifting of ledgers can be reconstructed for the stone slabs of the former factory at Palakollu within the Godavari–Krishna Delta, which had been deemed lost.[76] In the course of the Greifswald cemetery project, nine of them were identified within the park of the Victoria Jubilee Museum at Vijayawada. However, still in 1951, they were to be found on the supposedly original site at Palakollu.[77] Also the Dutch ledgers at Masulipatnam (Walandapalam) have obviously been shifted from their original position to the present site.

Generally, we may contend, that an orientation of the monuments different to the common east-westerly direction, remaining fragments or ledgers in quite unusual places or ledgers affixed to walls of churches and compound walls of burial grounds may bear witness for a later rearrangement. A lack of vertical monuments, which had been erected on most seventeenth- and eighteenth-century cemeteries might also be an indicator for a shifting of monuments, since vertical monuments—which were chiefly made of bricks—could not have been moved to another place without first destroying them.

In the course of the Greifswald cemetery project, about 20 sixteenth- to nineteenth-century European burial places in south India had been investigated. It was intended to select a representative choice of periods, regions and nationalities. However, due to the tremendously high number of surviving monuments, only a share of it could be studied and recorded comprehensively.[78] For identifying the very distinct characteristics of these individual burial places and to assign them to a distinct type, we have to ask for the circumstances and the time of their establishment, their specific geographical situation and for their internal structures.

The 'Garden' during the Factory Period

From the onset of the sixteenth century, small European trading settlements—the so-called factories—mushroomed all across the Indian subcontinent, especially along the shores of the Indian Ocean, along the River Hooghly in Bengal or in places further inland such as Patna. The factory site itself comprised rarely more than a small number of dwelling houses and godowns surrounded by a wooden fence or a compound wall, while a flagstaff and flag were usually not missing. Sometimes, a small kitchen garden as well as a light weaponry supplemented the ensemble of buildings. The factory plots were mainly situated within traditional Indian mercantile towns such as Masulipatnam, Cuddalore or Porto Novo (Parangipettai). In a few cases, Indo–European towns emerged out of these settlements as early as the sixteenth or seventeenth century such as Goa, Cochin, Madras or Danish Tranquebar.

As the number of European staff in the factories was small, burials were rare and there was no need for extensive European cemeteries. The small burial grounds were usually situated at some distance farther inland. This position chiefly resulted from the fact that the factories were largely placed close to the sea or rivers, rendering the sites prone to flooding. Usually, the Europeans found safer and more hygienic places to bury their dead a short distance away from the coast. The English burial place at Masulipatnam was, for instance, situated about 2 miles outside the town on a plot belonging to the English East India Company.[79] The first Dutch cemetery at Bimunipatnam (Walanda Bhumulu), accommodating Dutch graves from 1661 to 1719, was also situated at some distance outside the settlement, while only the younger cemetery from the latter half of the eighteenth century is placed much closer to the former Dutch fortress.[80] The same applies to South Coromandel, where notably the burial grounds of Pulicat, early Fort St. George, Porto Novo, Pondicherry, Cuddalore or Nagapattinam were established in some distance outside the factory grounds or fortresses.

In a somewhat euphemistical manner, these plots were commonly called 'Gardens'.[81] 'Gardens' usually served a double-purpose. They not only constituted a burial ground for the tiny group of Europeans in the factories, but simultaneously served as a recreational ground for weekend leisure and picnics. The English merchants at Masulipatnam, for instance, report on a cozy evening in 1679: 'In the evening we went and supd. at the Dutch garden which is about halfe a mile distance from the English garden, where the Dutch have two houses to which they often retire out of Towne for better aire which is alsoe much wanting in the English garden'.[82]

This seems to be quite strange today, which was obviously normal in the world of the European factories in south India during the seventeenth century: the combination of an airy leisure ground and a burial place.

The English merchant William Puckle noted the following in his diary on 1 August 1675 while staying at the English factory at Masulipatnam: 'M^{r}. Crandon lately dismissed his service of secretary at ye ffort, dyed intestate & was buryed in ye garden'.[83] Less than three weeks later, Puckle again records: 'An English bouldyer dyed and was buried in ye garden'.[84] The English merchant Streynsham Master likewise mentions the garden at Masulipatnam in 1679, however, without taking down its functioning as a burial ground: 'This evening we went to the English garden which is about two miles out of town over the long bridge, the water overflowing round the Towne now at spring tides'.[85] The English burial ground near Fort St. George was known as the 'Guava Garden'.

In some, however, quite unusual instances, factory burial grounds could at times be shifted inside factories or towns for safety reasons, which, for example, applies to the British burial grounds at Cuddalore. During the first half of the eighteenth century, two burial grounds had existed around the English factory—one north of the town, which simultaneously was also used by the Dutch (Sonaga Street Cemetery).[86] The second belonged to nearby Fort St. David and was situated northwest of that fort, with the oldest monument discovered around 1900 dating back to 1718.[87] In contrast to a general trend of shifting cemeteries outside the towns from the latter half of the eighteenth century, the Mysore Wars lead to the establishment of two new burial grounds inside Cuddalore very close to the British factory, one in Sloper Street and the other near the Mission Church.[88] However, interments in the old Sonaga Street Cemetery were resumed after the Battle of Seringapatnam and the fall of Mysore.

Today, only very few factory-cemeteries remain more or less undisturbed and yield a picture of their original size, such as the Binnenkerhof at Pulicat. When investigating the lifespan of a cemetery during the factory period, we have to take into account that the remaining monuments do not render an exact chronological framework. We do not know the number of lost monuments and of interments without a monument. Even at larger burial grounds, the ratio between the number of monuments and of interments according to the burial registers remains uneven.[89] Since almost no burial registers survive for the minor European factories, we cannot contend an exact lifespan of a distinct burial ground merely on the basis of the surviving monuments. Only a minimum period of usage may be identified.

According to the evidence rendered by Figures 11–17, the minimum lifetime of a 'garden' cemetery differed from a minimum of three decades (the Dutch burial ground at Golconda) to a maximum of 11 decades (at Masulipatnam). The figures show that the remaining monuments indicate a possible heyday of the burial grounds either in the latter half of the seventeenth century (Masulipatnam, Bimunipatnam, Golconda, Pulicat Buitenkerkhof and Binnenkerkhof) or during the first half of the eighteenth century (Karikop, Guava Garden).

The Guava Garden, however, seems to represent a special case. Even before Madras emerged as a major colonial town during the latter half of the eighteenth century, its European population (complemented by a large number of European and non-European soldiers) must have been substantial. While no burial records survive from the period between 1640 and 1680, about 3,650 persons were interred between 1680 and the abandonment of the 'Guava Garden' during the Seven Years' War.[90] A climax during the period 1711–20 can be grasped from both figures—the number of surviving monuments and the number of burials as well.

One most striking observation is the fact that the number of remaining monuments corresponds to the significance of a factory at a certain time. This notably applies to the Binnenkerkhof at Pulicat. Even if it is problematic to reconstruct an undisputable correlation between the number of burials and that of the surviving monuments, the figures clearly reveal that the largest number of monuments was obviously created during the latter half of the seventeenth century, while the number of surviving monuments from the eighteenth century is low and likewise displays a decreasing quality of workmanship. The 1660s and 1680s, similarly, proved to be the period that witnessed the largest net profits in Dutch Coromandel trade.[91]

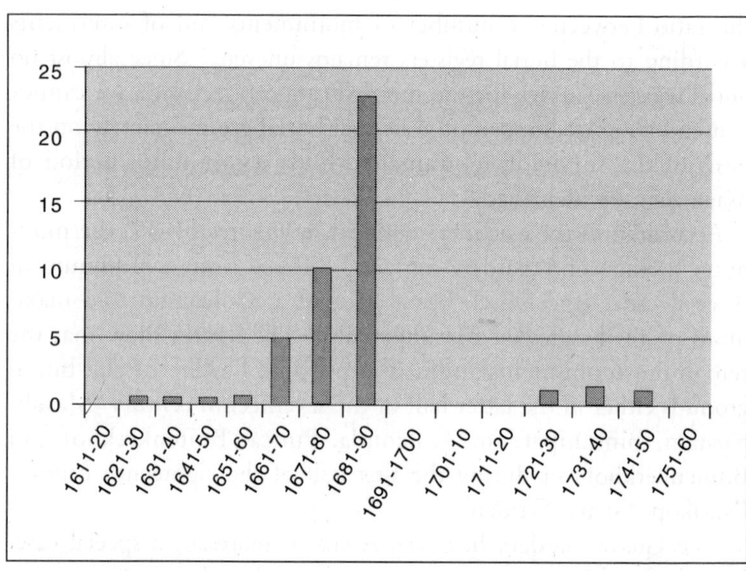

Figure 11: Number of surviving monuments at Pulicat, Buitenkerkhof

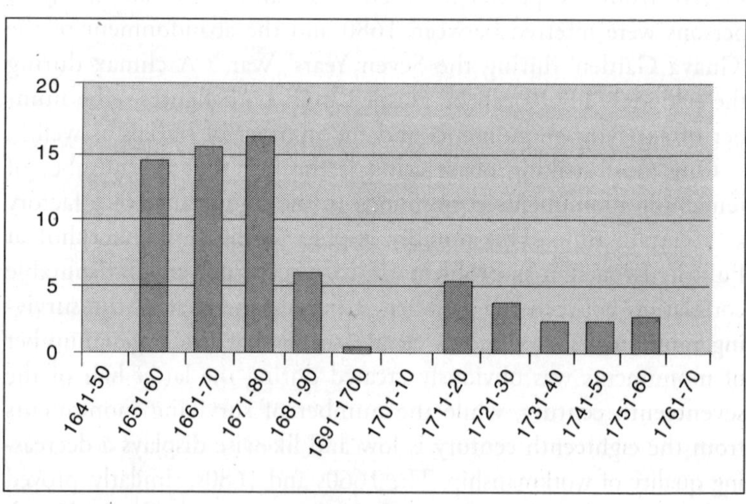

Figure 12: Number of surviving monuments at Pulicat, Binnenkerkhof

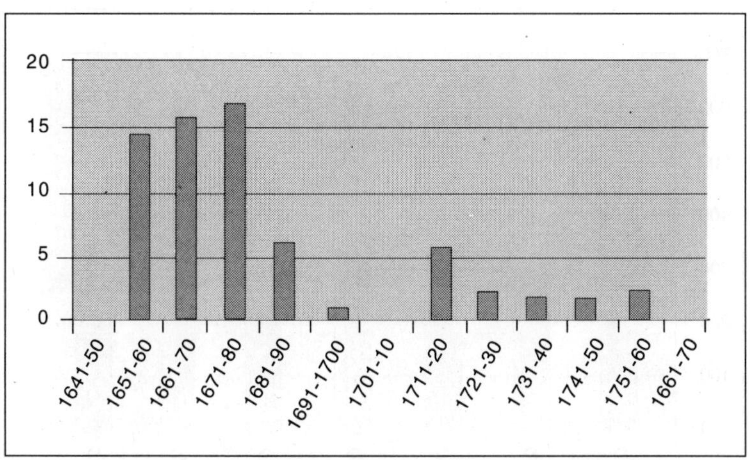

Figure 13: Number of surviving Dutch monuments at Masulipatnam

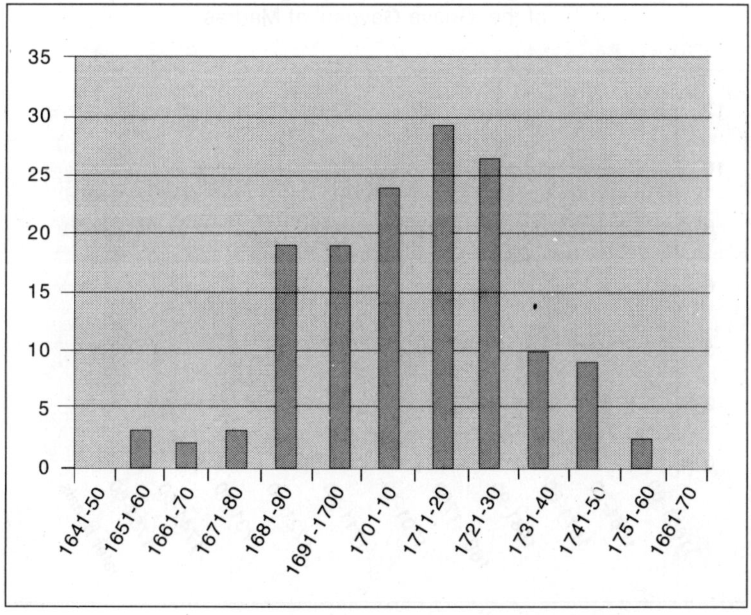

Figure 14: Number of surviving monuments of the 'Guava Garden' at Madras

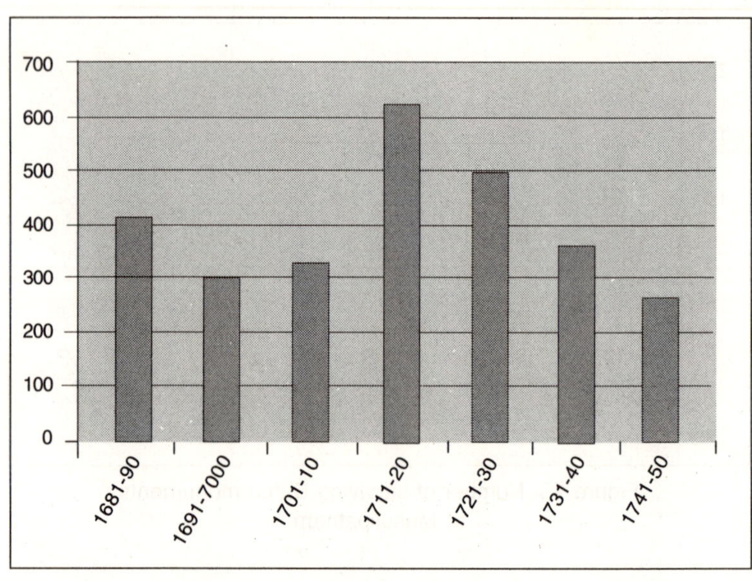

Figure 15: Number of burials according to the burial register of the 'Guava Gavden' at Madras

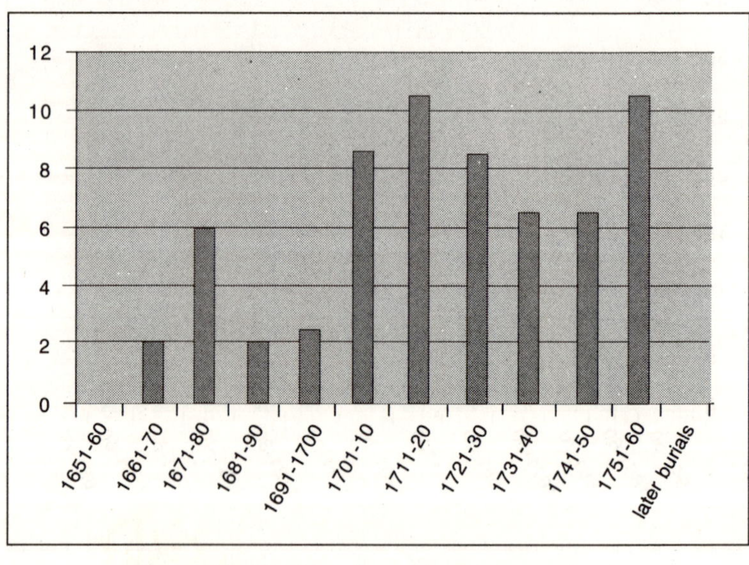

Figure 16: Number of surviving monuments at Karikop, Nagapattinam

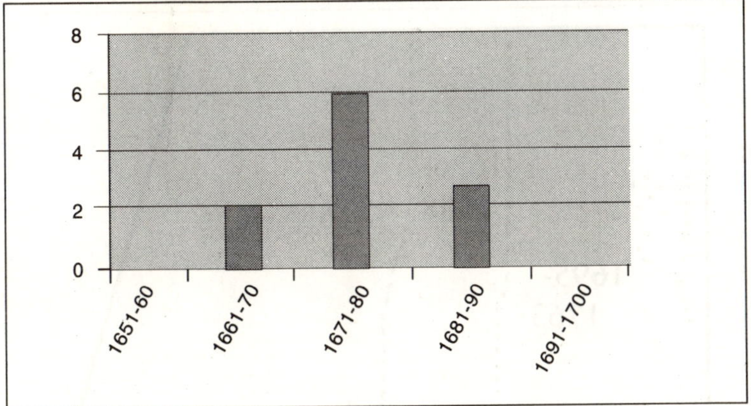

Figure 17: Number of surviving monuments at the Dutch burial ground at Golconda

We may well assume that the lifespan of a factory burial ground not only depended on the commercial success of a trading settlement, but also on the number of persons buried there (both factors, however, correspond to each other). A small ground, which could not be enlarged due to topographical conditions (such as swampy land), had to be fully closed or could remain open for only a very limited number of burials after the entire ground was covered with monuments. While graves of common Europeans without monuments might very likely have been replaced by new burials, it seems unlikely that monuments, which were mainly erected to commemorate members of the elite, would have been removed to yield space for new monuments. This situation particularly applies to the Binnenkerhof at Pulicat as can be studied from Figure 18.

An investigation of the stratigraphical development of the Binnenkerkhof suggests that the cemetery was gradually enlarged from east to west. Initially, the ground covered the eastern half of today's space, where we find the most representative monuments and a well of unknown age. From the latter half of the 1670s, the ground was obviously expanded. A final expansion took place from the very end of the seventeenth century. The utmost western line offering space for interments was reached latest during the 1780s—if not already around 1700 by the second extension.

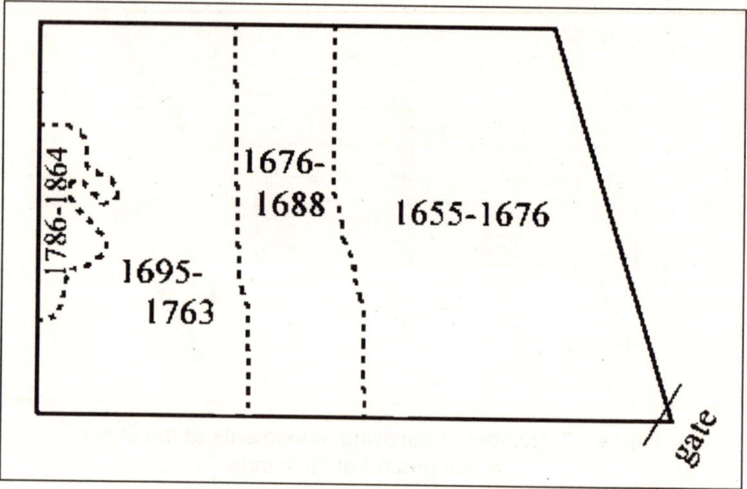

Figure 18: Temporal development of the Dutch Binnenkerkhof at Pulicat (not to scale)

During the latter half of the eighteenth century, the western part of the burial ground seems to have been increasingly congested and obviously could not be extended once more due to the swampy ground behind the compound. A number of late burials, until the 1860s, was carried out close to the western wall. However, the only chance of creating larger monuments was now to erect them within the oldest eastern sector, such as in the case of the representative monument of the Leembruggen family (1776–7) and the monument commemorating Sara Antonia de Goede (1793). We may well presume that some old monuments from the eastern portion (which could have been older than a century at this time) had crumbled and finally made space for new ones. Nevertheless, the comparatively low number of Dutch monuments from the eighteenth century likewise bears witness to the fact, that Pulicat's preeminent position in South Coromandel was now a thing of the past.

The material evidence leaves the impression that in some instances new burial grounds subsequently replaced the older ones. This assumption might have been the case in Bimunipatnam or Nagapattinam. However, only Pulicat, the headquarters of the

Dutch VOC in Coromandel, with two obviously little disturbed cemeteries, proves to be an unequivocal example. It is, however, to be perceived with all caution.

The figures shown in Figure 19 indicate that the Buitenkerkhof, also known as the Portuguese Cemetery, is obviously older. The oldest surviving monument dates back to 1631, two decades after the establishment of the Dutch factory. The number of surviving monuments significantly decreased from about the 1650s, while the Binnenkerkhof obviously gained even more importance by that time. The representative entrance gate of that cemetery was erected in 1656—an indicator of the assumption that this burial ground might have been established during that time. The establishment of a new burial ground at Pulicat with a representative entrance gate corresponds to the strengthened position of the VOC from mid-seventeenth century onwards due to the subsequent ousting of the Portuguese from south India.[92] However, even later, burials were carried out at the Buitenkerkhof.

In other cases, the use of an older burial ground abruptly ended, while virtually all interments took place on a new ground from a distinct date. This pattern mainly results from the impact of war,

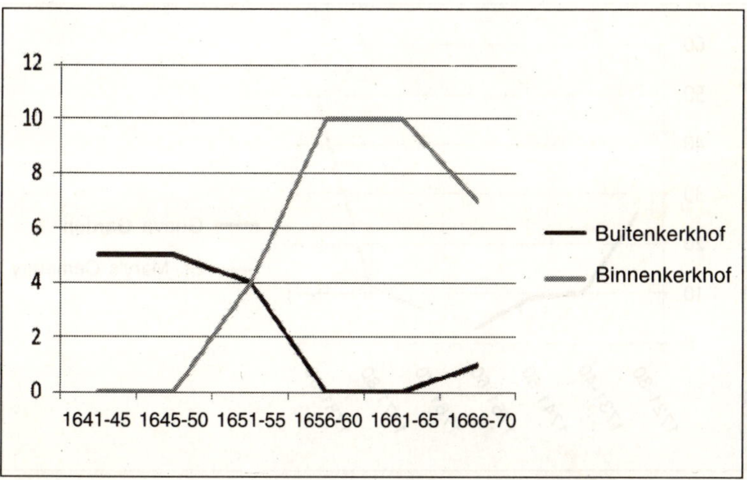

Figure 19: Number of remaining monuments at the Buitenkerkhof and the Binnenkerkhof of Pulicat (1630–1700)

when the traditional factory garden proved to be too unsafe or its ground was utilized for defence purposes. According to written sources, this was the fact for the English burial grounds at Cuddalore during the Seven Years' War (see earlier). The material evidence suggests a similar development of Guava Garden at Fort St. George (Figure 20).

At first, it can be observed, that the number of remaining monuments from the Guava Garden and St. Mary's Cemetery together was much lower from the 1740s to the 1760s, which might have resulted from the Anglo–French Wars and a subsequent decline in building activities. The most significant fact, however, is that no temporal overlap exists between both grounds. As the written sources clearly reveal, the Guava Garden had been levelled to the ground in 1757.[93] However, an exact date of shifting from the old ground to the new one is not recorded, and no break in the burial registers appear. The oldest recorded grave on the new St. Mary's Cemetery only dates back to 1763.[94]

Other former factory gardens survived the troublesome mid-eighteenth century and even the Napoleonic Wars. Nevertheless, notably the Dutch trading settlements and their adjacent burial

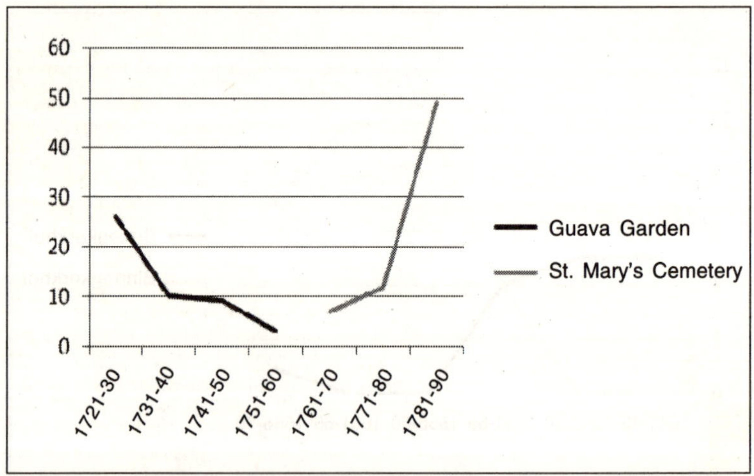

Figure 20: Number of remaining monuments from the 'Guava Garden' and St. Mary's Cemetery on the Island near Fort St. George (Madras)

grounds had witnessed a scattered fate from the Revolutionary Wars and the Napoleonic Wars onwards till the third decade of the nineteenth century. They had been captured by the British during the end of the eighteenth century. Even if their restoration was stipulated by the Peace of Amiens in 1802, the ongoing wars prevented their return. Only by 1819 most of them were returned to be handed over to the British again in 1825, in accordance with the Anglo–Dutch Treaty of 1824.[95] From about the mid-1820s, British burials were carried out on these grounds. In contrast to Bimunipatnam with a decreasing building activity, the transfer from Dutch to British burials seems to have been smooth and uninterrupted in Karikop at Nagapattinam.

The figures for Nagapattinam shown in Figure 21 clearly reveal that the members of the Dutch community were still buried at that place during the British occupation and (a very small number) even after the place had been transferred to the British in the 1820s.

Observations about people of different nationalities who were buried in Nagapattinam underline the impression that the multicultural and multidenominational colonial societies in south

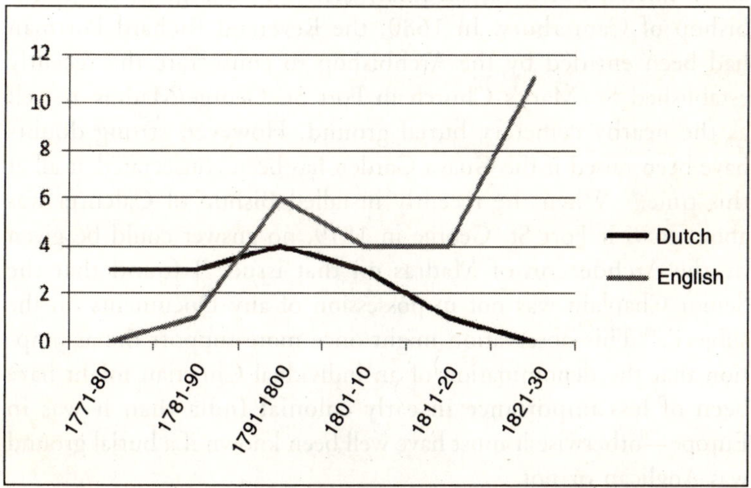

Figure 21: Dutch and British burials at Karikop, Nagapattinam (1770s to 1820s)

India significantly left their traces on the burial grounds. Is it, however, possible to identify a distinct policy of burial management regarding nationality and denomination during the factory period from the outset? Against this backdrop, it seems to be worthwhile investigating early Madras. Because the English East India Company at Fort St. George depended on the presence of local and European merchants of different nations and denominations, the interment of non-Anglicans obviously was not opposed by the Company. The remaining ledgers from the Guava Garden suggest that Portuguese Protestants like Francesco Marques (1687) or the Roman Catholic German Bernard Midon (1689), whose inscription displays the traditional Roman Catholic demand 'Orate pro eo' (pray for him), were buried here.[96] However, since the slabs had later been shifted to St. Mary's Church, their initial position inside the Guava Garden remains unclear.

Even if the Guava Garden was reserved for the Anglican community and a few other Christians, doubts might be raised if it was ever consecrated as an Anglican cemetery. No English bishop had resided in India before the second decade of the nineteenth century, while consecrations of burial grounds in India were officially carried out by subordinate clerics in charge of the Archbishop of Canterbury. In 1680, the Reverend Richard Portman had been entitled by the Archbishop to consecrate the recently established St. Mary's Church in Fort St. George/Madras as well as the nearby cemetery burial ground. However, strong doubts have been raised if the Guava Garden has been consecrated at all at this time.[97] When the recently installed Bishop of Calcutta was about to visit Fort St. George in 1819, no answer could be given by the Archdeacon of Madras on that issue: 'I found that the Senior Chaplain was not in possession of any Documents on the subject'.[98] This observation might once more support the assumption that the denomination of an individual Christian might have been of less importance in early colonial India than it was in Europe—otherwise it must have well been known if a burial ground was Anglican or not.

Nevertheless, Jews were not buried inside the Guava Garden, but in other places within the precincts of early Madras from the seventeenth century onwards. Since the East India Company claimed ownership of any freehold in the town, it was usually not willing to cede burial grounds to non-conformists on a permanent basis. Instead, land was leased out for a distinct period—for example, for fifteen years—under the precondition that monuments and surrounding walls were kept well-maintained. This, for instance, applies to the burial ground of the Jewish merchant Bartholomew Rodriguez, which was leased out in 1698 'as long as the heirs of Bartholomew Rodriguez kept the wall in repair. The ground was not to be alienated, sold, nor mortgaged; and if dilapidations were not made good, it was to revert to the Company.'[99]

Another example of a cemetery utilized by an international and multireligious European community is the burial ground of Porto Novo (Parangipettai), which accommodates the remains of a multinational trading community from the seventeenth to the nineteenth century. Next to Dutch and English merchants, we find the grave of the former Anglo–Danish resident at Porto Novo, Daniel Stephenson, who died in 1806.[100]

THE MODERN TOWN CEMETERY IN THE AGE OF TERRITORIAL EXPANSION

The territorial expansion of the British East India Company from the mid-eighteenth century brought about fundamental changes in the development of colonial settlements. Next to the already existing smaller factory sites and minor settlements like Tranquebar, virtual colonial cities like Madras or Cochin arose out of formerly small Indo–European towns. The number of Europeans grew due to an increase in immigration, a growing presence of European women and an increasing birth rate. This structural change is also mirrored by a steadily rising number of deaths, which notably applies to ever-growing Madras.

The number of burials at Madras was always fluctuating (see Figure 22). Nevertheless, a significant upward trend is noticeable from the 1750s onwards. While the annual number of burials hardly reached 50 before 1750, it later rose to 150–200. This fundamental change demanded an increasing institutionalization

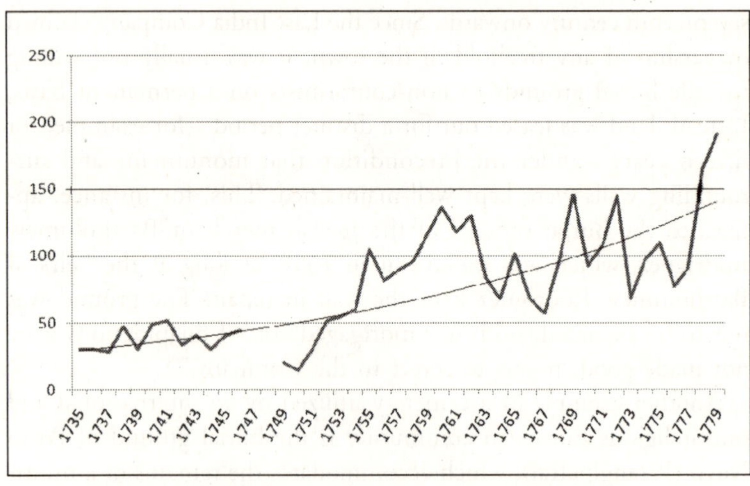

Figure 22: Annual number of burials at Guava Garden and St. Mary's Cemetery, Madras (1735–79)

and professionalization of cemetery management. Furthermore, the structure of the European cemeteries also simultaneously changed. On the one hand, the traditional factory cemetery or 'garden' gradually disappeared or was converted into a larger town cemetery (Nagapattinam), while on the other hand, new town or new parochial cemeteries were established in south India.

It was notably South Park Street Cemetery at Calcutta which served as a model for other burial grounds not only in India but also in Europe (Plate 7). Founded in 1767, it was established outside the precincts of colonial Calcutta to evade health hazards emanating from burials inside the town in a tropical climate. Because it was created on a formerly empty space, the founders did not have to consider an older topography, but could create a geometrical grid-pattern which yielded abundant space for the erection of representative monuments. Already by 1812, the visitor encountered 'many acres covered so thick with columns, urns and obelisks that there scarcely seems to be room for another, . . . it is like a city of the dead'.[101]

Another trend commenced at the onset of the nineteenth century and brought forward a legal basis as well as a democratization of funerary culture in Europe and the colonial world. New legal frameworks established from Napoleonic times confined interments to the large cemeteries outside the towns. Burials inside churches were henceforth prohibited. While most deceased persons were never commemorated by a monument before, the tomb monuments now generally became smaller and were thus affordable to the rising middle classes—a trend which came up in Europe and in India alike.[102]

The modern European town cemeteries of south India were of less grandeur than the South Park Street Cemetery at Calcutta, but they nevertheless displayed a similar topography. First, the new burial grounds were initially situated outside the ever-growing towns, such as in the case of Madras (St. Mary's Cemetery, see Plate 8) or Pondicherry (Cholas Nagar, see Plate 9). Second, they were not only characterized by geometrical structures, but sometimes also by neo-Gothic entrance gates with watchmen's premises, which still survive in Madras (St. Mary's and Kilpauk). New cemeteries with similar features were increasingly established further inland such as in Madurai, Thiruchirapalli (churchyard of Anglican St. John's and Christ Church, of Roman Catholic St. Mary's Church and the so-called Chintámani Cemetery).[103] From the 1820s, new burial grounds were likewise founded near the hill stations of the Nilgiris (Kotagiri, Ootacamund, Coonoor).

In other instances, older cemeteries from the factory period remained near the factory or fortress, but were expanded, which applies to Tranquebar (Plate 10) and Nagapattinam (Karikop). While Tranquebar's Nyegade Kirkegaard must gradually have been expanded towards the north during the nineteenth century, Karikop was expanded towards the west during the same period.

Where space was available, the new burial grounds were at times further extended, which can be reconstructed from the written sources as well as from the position of the surviving monuments. The new St. Mary's Cemetery on the Island near Fort St. George proved to be too small just less than four decades after its foundation. In contrast to the suggestion of the local vestry to pull down a nearby powder magazine, it was obviously expanded into another southern direction around 1800. Further extensions were carried out at the western and northern sides.[104] From the 1820s, even these extensions proved insufficient and new cemeteries were established as near St. Matthias' Church at Vepery, which was opened in 1826, and later the Kilpauk Cemetery.[105]

The development of St. George's cemetery at Madurai renders an excellent example of spatial development in the course of time. (Figure 23).

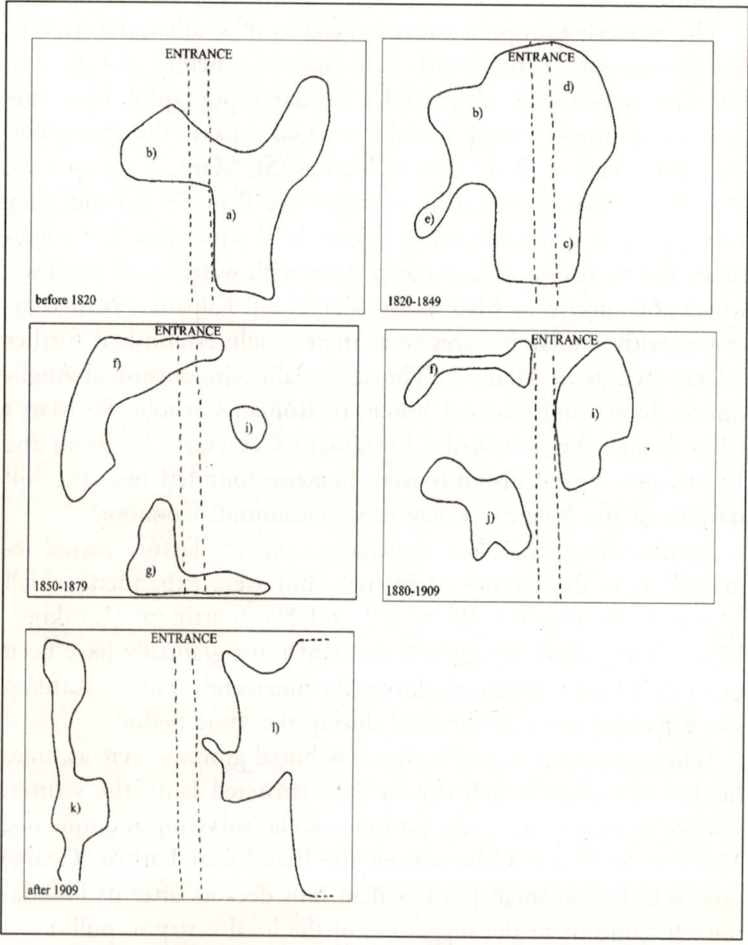

Figure 23: Development of St. George's Cemetery, Madurai (eighteenth to twentieth centuries), not to scale

Plate 1: Inscription-plaques as sources for demographical studies. An example from the French Cemetery at Cholas Nagar, Pondicherry

Plate 2: Former 'Guava Garden', Madras, Yale-monument

Plate 3: Former 'Guava Garden', Madras, surviving foundations of ledgers

Plate 4: European Cemetery at Porto Novo, derelict monuments

Plate 5: Binnenkerkhof, Pulicat

Plate 6: Transferred stone slabs from the former 'Guava Garden' at St. Mary's Church, Madras

Plate 7: South Park Street Cemetery, Calcutta

Plate 8: St. Mary's Cemetery, Madras

Plate 9: French Cemetery at Cholas Nagar, Pondicherry

Plate 10: Nyegade Kirkegaard, Tranquebar

Plate 11: European Cemetery, Kotagiri, the oldest surviving European monuments in the Nilgiris

Plate 12: St. Stephen's Church Cemetery, Ootacamund

Plate 13: Walandapalam, Masulipatnam, semi-finished ledger

Plate 14: Nyegade Kirkegaard, Tranquebar, signature of W. Johnson, sculptor at Thiruchirapalli

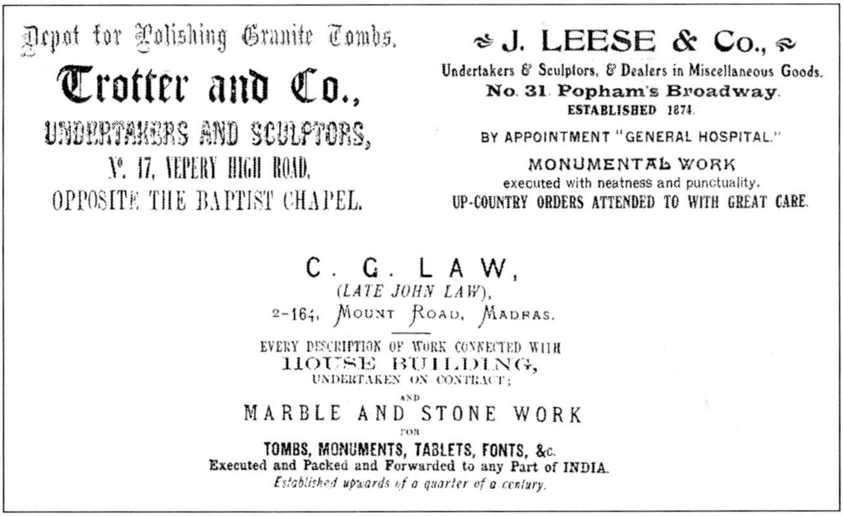

Depot for Polishing Granite Tombs.

Trotter and Co.,

UNDERTAKERS AND SCULPTORS,

No. 17, VEPERY HIGH ROAD,

OPPOSITE THE BAPTIST CHAPEL.

J. LEESE & Co.,

Undertakers & Sculptors, & Dealers in Miscellaneous Goods.

No. 31. Popham's Broadway.

ESTABLISHED 1874.

BY APPOINTMENT "GENERAL HOSPITAL."

MONUMENTAL WORK

executed with neatness and punctuality.

UP-COUNTRY ORDERS ATTENDED TO WITH GREAT CARE.

C. G. LAW,

(LATE JOHN LAW),

2-164, Mount Road, Madras.

EVERY DESCRIPTION OF WORK CONNECTED WITH

HOUSE BUILDING,

UNDERTAKEN ON CONTRACT;

AND

MARBLE AND STONE WORK

FOR

TOMBS, MONUMENTS, TABLETS, FONTS, &c.

Executed and Packed and Forwarded to any Part of INDIA.

Established upwards of a quarter of a century.

Plate 15: Undertakers' advertisements, Madras (Madras Almanac and Compendium of Intelligence, Madras 1835–70)

Plate 16: Church of St. Francis of Assisi, Old Goa, family tomb of Jo o Ruiz (1649)

Plate 17: Bom Jesus, Old Goa, tomb of Francis Xavier (*c.* 1635–41)

Plate 18: Dutch Cemetery Palakollu (today at the Victoria Jubilee Museum, Vijayawada), monument of Lambert Wildelandt (d. 1681), an example of elaborate Indo-Dutch funerary sculpturing

Plate 19: Binnenkerkhof, Pulicat, monument of Abraham Mendis (d. 1684)

Plate 20: Buitenkerkhof, Pulicat, child of Willem Tack (d. 1644), ledger without border decoration

Plate 21: Binnenkerkhof, Pulicat, Elysabeth Pit, child (d. 1656), example of early Dutch border decoration

Plate 22: Oude Kerkhof, Sadras, family monument van den Briel (1687–1705), example of late-seventeenth-century border decoration

Plate 23: Oude Kerkhof, Sadras, Jan Jacob Topander (d. 1757), Baroque-inspired mid-eighteenth-century border decoration

Plate 24: Binnenkerkhof, Pulicat, monument of Anna Margaretha Möller (d. 1737)

Plate 25: French Cemetery at Cholas Nagar, Pondicherry, early-nineteenth-century monument

Plate 26: Nyegade Kirkegaard, Tranquebar, undated monument in Indo-European hybrid style

Plate 27: Kilpauk Cemetery, Madras, Neo-Gothic entrance gate

A study of the development of the cemetery along the main axis from the main entrance in the north towards the south shows an entirely different picture compared to the linear development of the Binnenkerkhof at Pulicat (Figure 18). Its development can rather be compared to the different layers on an onion from its core to the outer skin. The oldest layer from before 1820 (and with the oldest surviving grave from 1773) in the south constitutes the core situated mainly east of the main axis (a), however, with a branch stretching across towards the west (b). The second stage describes the development between the 1820s and the 1840s. Only to a small degree, the areas covered by graves now correspond to the area of the first period, chiefly southeast of the main axis (c) and on the branch in the west (b). On the other hand, new areas are now covered in the north adjacent to the present main entrance (d) and a thin branch stretching towards the southwest (e). It seems as if the core area of St. George's Cemetery was now entirely covered by graves and no more space was available, so new areas in the periphery were later developed: in the northwest (f), in the south (g) and a small plot in the centre of the eastern portion (i) (1850–79). During the fourth period (1880–1909), the latter portion (i) was extended and a new area in the southwest (j) was developed, while bodies were simultaneously being interred in a small portion in the northwest, where interments had already taken place in period 3 (f). Period 5 (after 1909) shows a final stage of development in the periphery of the far west (k) and towards the east (l), developing new areas during the twentieth century.

The establishment of modern town cemeteries with an even larger number of burials brought about a remarkable professionalization of financial, legal and administrative matters. It is not to be examined, from which time exactly charges for burials started being levied and from when cemetery regulations were imposed on the European cemeteries in south India. However, during the final decades of the eighteenth century, this issue obviously gained more importance. The church accounts from the Zion Church of Tranquebar, for instance, record a regular income for the church treasury from the fees levied from baptisms, weddings and burials from 1781 onwards, burials obviously being the most profitable source of income (see Chapter 1).

From 1785 onwards, the question regarding fees became a more delicate issue at Fort St. George as well. At the onset of that year, the local Vestry submitted a proposal to the government for a regulation of fees, which was subsequently approved and signed by the Governor without changes. The basic idea of this new scheme was that it was socially acceptable. Two different levels of fees were to be introduced according to wealth and social status:

> It is also considered that the fees should be adapted to the circumstances of the individuals in the society, and shall be proportionate to their condition. For this purpose parishioners are divided into two classes, superior rank and inferior rank, and it is left to the discretion of the ministers to determine the class to which it belongs.[106]

It was furthermore stipulated, that the corpse of the deceased endowed with the 'best pall' would automatically be allotted to the superior and more expensive rank. A burial of inferior rank would cost 5 pagodas, while that of a superior rank would be as twice as much.[107] Also, the erection of a monument on St. Mary's Cemetery near Fort St. George was not free of charge from 1785 onwards. In the regulations approved during that year, 20 pagodas would be charged for a monument erected for someone allotted to a superior rank; for somebody from the inferior rank it was 10 pagodas, apart from the expenses spent for the erection of the monument. These figures clearly reveal the fact that erecting a monument was, during late eighteenth century, a costly affair which only a few could afford in commemoration of the deceased.[108]

A quarter of the fees levied was to be passed in the hands of the English Charity School Fund at Madras.[109] Before 1805, the remaining sums flooded to the pocket of the Vestries and the ministers.[110] In 1805, all Vestries were dissolved in the course of a church reform in British India, and the cemeteries were now directly subordinated to the colonial government. After the Vestries were dissolved and administration of the churches and burial grounds handed over to the East India Company, deliberate discussions on future cemetery rules were held. This development can be regarded as an indicator of an increasing institutionalization and professionalization of funeral services (similar to the development in Europe in the wake of the Napoleonic reforms). The first drafts were sketched by individual church committees and submitted to the government at Fort St. George for being sanctioned. A very elaborate draft was, for example, submitted by the just recently established St. George Church (Madras) in 1818: The administrative basis for interment ought to be the allocation of a certain district in town to a cemetery—exceptions, however, would be permitted against the payment of a fee. Furthermore, the situation, extent and height of the monuments was fixed to render a geometrical appearance to the burial ground. Daytime interment was stipulated in accordance to the already existing traditions for the early morning (6.30 a.m.) and late afternoon (5.30 p.m.). An additional source of income was hoped to be secured by offering the opportunity to purchase distinct plots for future single or family burials, well in advance. Finally, a regular fee was fixed.[111]

An increasing sense for such regulations subsequently gave rise to some general deliberations on uniform rules by the Bishop of Calcutta 'having employed . . . his intention of making some general regulations regarding funeral fees and other matters connected with funerals' in 1818.[112] The outcome of these deliberations were general burial rules issued by the Bishop of Calcutta and later by the Bishop of Madras,[113] mainly embarking on the early drafts of the individual church committees.[114]

From now onwards, the situation, shape and size of the monument was no more subject to individual decision of the relatives or heirs of the deceased. They were laid down in cemetery rules instead. The draft for St. George's Cathedral Cemetery from 1818 thus stipulates:

> Graves shall in all cases be formed with particular reference to the letters on the wall on the one side, and to the figures on the other, so that a straight line drawn from one and the other shall pass over the middle of the grave.
>
> The space allotted for a grave and monument shall not exceed 10 feet by 6 from which one foot shall be left on each side, for a sufficient interval between the graves.
>
> Every grave shall be sunk to the depth of 6 feet and no monument shall be allowed to exceed 12 feet in height.[115]

Such pattern of letters and figures still survives in a number of European nineteenth-century burial grounds in south India such as in Madras, Madurai, Ootacamund and Kotagiri. Round, plastered markers to indicate the lines on which the monuments were to be oriented still survive on one of the walls of the European cemetery in Kotagiri from about the 1930s.

From 1805, any alteration in the burial grounds or inside the churches had to be sanctioned by the government at Fort St. George as well. Epitaphs to be affixed inside the churches were examined by the church committees in the workshops of the sculptors, and their assessment was sent to the government for final approval.[116]

A striking professionalism is to be witnessed regarding the parish books as well. From late eighteenth century, it was regularly deplored by the government at Fort St. George that entries into the parish books had become irregular in the British outstations of south India. In 1800, it was decided by the directors that copies of all parish books and current entries were to be sent to Madras on a regular basis.[117] The proper maintenance of parish books was now increasingly regarded as being of legal significance. This new trend lead to distinct rules as to how to record the entries of the burial registers as, for example, stipulated by the *Revised Rules for the Guidance of Chaplains* from 2 November 1832: 'Form of the Register for Burials. On this (day of the month and year) A. (if an infant add Son or Daughter of) A. of (place or abode, profession or business) and B. his wife aged . . . years, was buried at (Chaplaincy). By me (C.) Chaplain at. . . .'[118]

As during the preceding factory period, the town cemeteries of the late eighteenth and nineteenth century in south India still accommodated the bodies of persons of different denominations. This especially applies to smaller towns, where only one or two multidenominational burial grounds could be maintained, such as in the case of the European cemetery at Nellore with both Protestant and Catholic burials.[119] During the nineteenth century, the colonial British authorities still did not find an obstacle in providing space for interments of non-Anglicans. This policy notably transpires from a dispatch of the government at Fort St. George in 1841: 'We think it very desirable that on occasions of enclosing grounds for cemeteries a portion of it should in every case be set apart for parties, being Christians, who may differ in their faith from the Church of England'.[120] Cemeteries of places with a large multidenominational European population like cantonments could well have been divided into distinct Anglican and Roman Catholic portions, such as the two European cemeteries at Seringapatnam.[121] The Danes obviously proved to be less liberal as they maintained a separate Catholic cemetery, which had existed already during the seventeenth century and which was still in use in the nineteenth century.[122]

Special sites were usually designated for victims of suicide, either inside or outside the cemetery. At Tranquebar, for instance, the bodies of such people were buried in the western corner of the Nyegade Kirkegaard.[123] However, to get a place secured inside the walls of the cemetery, the victim at least needed to have committed suicide in a state of absent mindedness ('i vildelse'), which was thoroughly recorded in Tranquebar's burial register.

The European's Indian lovers—or 'beebee' as they were called—was usually denied grave in a European cemetery.[124] Only in a very few cases, non-Europeans were buried in European cemeteries. They were mainly Armenian merchants or Christian servants of the Europeans such as a 'black cook by name Abraham Mooshøj' from the ship *Mount Vernon*—very likely a Christian—who was buried at Tranquebar in 1798.[125] The burials of European servants with a monument in town cemeteries became more frequent only during the nineteenth century. However, even if their worldly merits and virtues were applauded by a small number of inscriptions, they were clearly classified as 'subordinates' by the commissioner of the monument. This applies to Joanna Frantz, who died in 1847 at the age of 22 years and was buried in St. Mary's Cemetery at Madras. The inscription of her monument reads: 'She was a truly good and valuable servant. / And her excellent qualities gained her universal esteem. / This Monument is erected in testimony / at the great regard of one whom she served / with strict fidelity and strong attachment. / For a period of ten years.' During the first half of the nineteenth century, employing a female servant of the age of 12 obviously was not an offence.

A quite extraordinary story is connected with the founding of St. Mary's Church at Masulipatnam with its adjacent churchyard—the third English burial ground in the town after the 'English Garden' and a garrison cemetery, which was in use from 1787 to 1834. The church had initially been established as a chapel for the interment of the Indian mistress of Major-General John Pater. At first the body of the deceased had been embalmed and placed in a coffin with a glass lid in the veranda of his house. Two years later, in 1811, Pater was entitled to construct a chapel to accommodate the earthly remains of his mistress, which simultaneously was used for public service from 1815 onwards. An English churchyard around the building was established soon after.[126]

Burial Grounds of the Hill Stations

From the 1820s, a number of hill stations emerged in the Eastern and Western Ghats and notably in the Nilgiris. For a long time, the Nilgiris or the 'Blue Mountains' as it was called were more or less unknown to the Europeans. Only the defeat of Mysore in the Battle of Seringapatnam and the subsequent cession of the territory of Mysore including the Nilgiris to the British rendered this mountain range more interesting to the Europeans. In 1821, John Sullivan, the Collector of Coimbatore, lead an expedition to the mountains with a small travelling company. He climbed up the narrow, steep ghats of the eastern slope to reach a place where later European Kotagiri was to emerge. Finally, he proceeded to the heart of the mountains to a plot of land which the local hill tribes called Wytacamund, which was later converted by Europeans to Ootacamund. To Sullivan's amazement, the climate was quite similar to Europe, with cool summers and frost during winter time though it was located only a few hundred kilometres north of the equator. It was soon discovered that these mountains were an ideal place for recouping or to spend summer vacations. Sanatoriums, hotels, clubs and churches sprung up in Ootacamund, Kotagiri and Coonoor within one or two decades, and European cemeteries as well.

In the beginning of the European history of the Nilgiris, it seems to be quite accidental that cemeteries adjacent to hill stations were established in a distinct spot. Sometimes, the scattered graves of the earliest travellers were taken as a point of reference, even if this spot later proved to be in a very remote part of the settlement. This, for instance, applies to the European cemetery in Kotagiri (Plate 11):

> The European cemetery lies at the other end of the station, on a spur overlooking Dimhatti. It is said that this odd and out-of-the-way site was fixed by the accident that in the very early days of the station an officer who had pitched his tents there died and was buried in front of them. Subsequent graves were placed alongside his, and the spot became the recognized cemetery.[127]

Later, from the 1830s, geometrical town cemeteries emerged near Ootacamund (Plate 12), Coonoor and other places in the Nilgiris like Keti with its station founded by the Basle missionaries. St. Stephen's Cemetery at Ootacamund (Udhagamandalam/ Ooty) is still an exceptionally beautiful place climbing up a hill behind St. Stephen's Church. Due to the fact that the European community in Ootacamund survived Independence for decades, it is still an open cemetery and still used for burying the remains of the members of the tiny European community there. Its development started during the 1820s with the oldest graves being placed directly behind the church. Extensions were carried out on both sides during the 1840s and 1850s and upwards the hill towards the back from the 1870s onwards. Interestingly, a separate portion for infant and child burials seems to have been provided from the 1840s in the upper part of the ground at some distance from the other graves.

Cantonments and War Graves

The British territorial expansion and the frequent wars between British, French and local Indian troops brought an increasing number of European soldiers to India. The old burial grounds within the precincts of British forts soon became too small in the course of the expansion of the garrisons, notably during the nineteenth century. A burial ground had been, for instance, established in the British Fort at Bangalore in 1791. Already eighteen years later, the available space did not prove to be sufficient and a new cantonment-cemetery had to be founded, which was, however, closed down in 1868.[128] Sometimes the initial choice of a ground for a burial site in recently established military camps or forts was not satisfactory due to a lack of knowledge of the local topography. Soon after the foundation of the (old) burial ground near St. John's Church at Secunderabad, it was, for instance, discovered that it converted into a swamp during the rainy season. However, after the first corpses have been buried there, the local authorities did not feel inclined to change the situation till some time later.

Where space permitted, the social order and different military ranks were observed on the burial grounds of the cantonments within British India. When Christ Church inside the fort of Thiruchirapalli had been opened with its adjoining burial ground in 1766, interments were reserved only for high-ranking officers and distinguished civilians. Common soldiers were buried at some distance outside the fort in a place called Chintámani. When cavalry and infantry moved from the fort itself to an open space outside the town, a new cemetery was established at the village Warriore.[129]

Similar to the factory cemeteries, cantonment and war cemeteries boast the remains of a multireligious and multinational European community. A number of Swiss mercenaries were buried at Seringapatnam during the military encounters with Tipu Sultan of Mysore in 1799. Most of them had served in the regiment raised by Comte du Meuron at Neufchaftel to be employed by the VOC in the Cape Colony and later by the British in Ceylon and south India.[130]

While British cantonment-cemeteries are well known and remain well maintained till today (such as the war grave portion of St. Mary's Cemetery in Madras), almost nothing remains of the French military burial grounds. In 1750, for instance, General de Bussy had succeeded in conquering the fortified town of Gingee from the Nawab of Arcot. For almost a decade it was in the hands of French troops, and it was endeavoured to modernize the fortification according to modern Western standards. A number of French soldiers who very likely had lost their lives here were supposedly buried in a piece of ground northeast of the so-called Royal Battery.

Only two monuments commemorating a French missionary and his Indian catechist have survived on this spot.[131]

The Interments Inside Churches

The longest tradition of interring the dead inside churches was maintained by the Portuguese. Even the tiny sixteenth-century communities like those of Pulicat, Tranquebar and Devanampattinam established churches.[132] Interment *intra muros* had not always been accepted even by the Roman Catholic Church. A ban was first imposed by the Council of Braga in 563. It was repeated by many ensuing settlements—a clear indicator of the fact that the ban was frequently violated. Everyday customs and the belief of the benefit to be put to rest as close to the altar and the remains of the saints as possible, proved to be more enduring than the official policy of the church.[133] In Europe, the medieval ban of burials inside churches was particularly repeated and renewed during the sixteenth and seventeenth centuries in the period of confessionalization.[134] However, even the Roman Catholic Church admitted exemptions such as for priests and church patrons or meritorious laics, as stipulated, for instance, by the Councils of Rouen (1581) and Reims (1683).[135] In fact, the ban was never fully observed, neither in Catholic nor in Reformed or Lutheran churches until the end of the eighteenth century.[136] A large number of ledgers inside many churches in Europe, especially in the Netherlands, bear witness to this fact. The same applies to south India as well.

A classic example of the interment of bodies inside Catholic churches in south India is, next to Goa, St. Francis Church in Cochin, initially called St. Anthony Church. This church was erected by Franciscan friars as their community's chapel at the onset of the sixteenth century. In 1524, Vasco da Gama was buried inside the church until his earthly remains found a final resting place in Lisbon 14 years later. Other interments were to follow. After the Dutch had occupied the town in 1663, it was converted into a Calvinist church. Despite an entirely different denomination, the Dutch left the Portuguese ledgers on the church floor and buried the Calvinist members of their own social elite next to their Catholic predecessors. While the Roman Catholic denomination was officially denied by the Dutch, they obviously simultaneously displayed a sense of respect towards the social status of the deceased. Even afterwards, the bodies of individiaul Portuguese were buried here (Figure 24). The building itself remained well maintained and later got a new roof.[137] Even after Cochin's surrender to the British in 1795, the church remained Dutch for nine more years, until it became Anglican. Most likely, it was renamed St. Francis during the second half of the nineteenth century. Around 1900 the Portuguese and Dutch ledgers were removed from the floor and fixed along the northern and southern side walls inside the building for a better maintenance. Today, the building is maintained by the Church of South India (CSI).

Interments inside Anglican churches were initially not permitted. When the new St. Mary's Church at Fort St. George was about to be consecrated at the end of the seventeenth century, the Bishop of London announced '. . . notwithstanding that for the future noe corps may be interred within the said church or in the Churchyard adjoining thereunto'.[138] Such ban of intra-mural interments

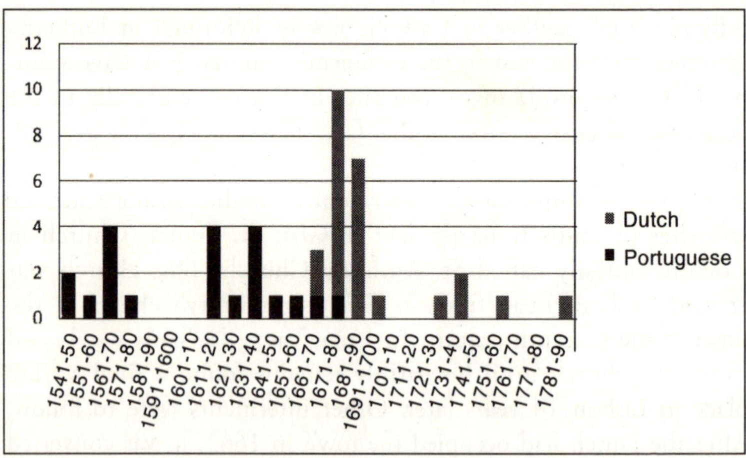

Figure 24: Portuguese and Dutch ledgers inside St. Francis Church, Cochin[139]

and burials within the churchyard of St. Mary's clearly unveils the contemporary—at least official—attitude towards funerals in post-Reformation England. From the onset of the Reformation, a commemorative prayer for the benefit of the soul of the deceased close to the grave, the nearby altar and the relics of the saints did not any more correspond to the official theology. Radical Protestants would entirely refuse the burial in consecrated soil as being superstitious.[140] Furthermore, an increasing sense for public health and a salubrious environment prevented the church authorities from admitting intra-mural interments. On the contrary, extra-parochial cemeteries outside the precincts of London were founded from the 1560s, such as the New Churchyard outside Bishopsgate as the first of a number of similar burial grounds.[141] Such official notions were without doubt transferred to the English settlements in India, when the first churches were erected and larger burial grounds had to be established.

However, a new sense of worldliness and representation attributed to funeral and commemoration was mirrored by a still-existing desire for an intra-mural interment. The burial within the church would now reflect the elites' reputation, social distinction and the wealth of the deceased. This dichotomy between official policy and private effort often gave rise to a deliberate discussion at home and in India. In the latter half of the eighteenth century, the ban on interment inside St. Mary's at Fort St. George seems to have been fallen into disuse. A virtual precedent was set, when the Right Hon. Lord Pigot was buried inside the church in 1777, who was furthermore commemorated by a stone slab and an escutcheon on a wall inside the building. This exception was carried out at the Lord's son-in-law Edward Monckton bidding, which was approved by the local church authorities 'in consideration of His Lordship's distinguished character and the essential services he has rendered the public'.[142] Later, the Vestry felt compelled to claim that it was 'necessary to remark that this is not to be looked upon as a precedent to any future interment'.[143] After Sir Eyre Coote, who had successfully defeated the French in south India during the Seven Years' War, had died in April 1783, another interment *intra muros* could not be denied, for

> ... the service of Sir Eyre Coote having not only obtained him the repeated applause and thanks of this country but made the most grateful impression on the mind of every individual here, who are sensible to his great exertions. . . .[144]

Even if the corpse of Sir Eyre Coote remained inside the church for only about a year, to be later transferred to England, this example clearly reveals, that an interment inside the church building in the meantime emerged as a means to display a distinguished person's social, political or military status. The Vestry of St. Mary's Church obviously soon after perceived that it would be difficult to contain such a trend if it once commenced. In 1786 and 1787, applications of two high-ranking soldiers were refused. Only when the government at Fort St. George applied for the interment of Colonel Moorhouse, who had been killed in a military attack at Bangalore in 1791, the Vestry had no way but to give in, because the government initially threatened to involve Governor-General Cornwallis into this matter.[145] From that time onwards, intra mural interments were unofficially allowed for high-ranking civilians or soldiers such as Governors, Puisne Judges, Members of the Council, Commanders-in-Chief and their wives and children. However, between 1777 and 1875 only 14 interments inside St. Mary's Church took place.[146]

The Vestries of churches outstations obviously pursued a more liberal policy towards this issue—very likely due to the much smaller European population and a lesser pressure of the far distant church authorities. When Christ Church was opened inside the Fort of Thiruchirapalli in 1766, burials intra-muros were officially permitted by the local Vestry from the outset. Until 1797, 13 interments took place inside the church, but none, however, during the nineteenth century. This development may serve as an indicator, that the grip of the central church authorities on local church policy became tighter after 1800. At Thiruchirapalli, mainly high-ranking officers with their wives and children were buried inside the church.[147] The same applies to St. Peter's Church at Tanjore, where intra-mural burials were permitted from the 1780s; but only two were ever carried out (1780, 1791).[148]

Due to the absence of bishops, some churches remained unconsecrated, which obviously yielded an opportunity for intra-mural interments. After, for example, Christ Church in the Old Town of Cuddalore had been erected and dedicated in 1767, 18 interments took place inside the building. This practice came to an end only after the church was consecrated by Bishop Spencer in 1845, except for one final exception in 1847.[149] Nevertheless, the number of burials inside churches generally decreased during the first half of the nineteenth century. Churches erected during this period or later were not any more earmarked for that purpose such as St. Mary's Church at Arcot (Ranipett), which was erected in 1814–15.[150]

Scattered Monuments

Graves alongside the dusty roads of South Asia are quite a common feature of European burial practice from the outset of European presence in Asia. It seems likely that many deceased were never commemorated by a monument, such as a common sailor of the VOC who had died on a march along the Ceylonese coast in 1671. It is reported that a pit was dug in a hurry and the corpse buried there. Its only protection were thorns to cover the grave to keep away wild animals.[151] The likeliness of dying far away from a cemetery was already taken into account by a number of wills, which—for instance—transpires from the will of Sergeant George Boyd (1818): '. . . and [I] direct my body to be interred by my executors, in Christian burial ground, or, as circumstances will admit.'[152]

While the dispersed grave only happened to be dug due to the long distance to a proper, if not consecrated, burial ground, a small number of very distinguished persons preferred a monument outside the public cemetery on a private ground or inside a park, in accordance to eighteenth-century European sense for Romanticism. One of them was the surgeon and scientist Edmund Bulkeley, who had died in 1713 and was buried in the so-called 'Physic Garden'. This garden had been founded by Bulkeley himself and was situated about half a kilometre west of Fort St. George.[153]

The special attachment of a deceased to an individual site could have given rise to the creation of a monument on a remote place.

This, for example, applies to William French of the British East India Company, who was not only buried in the Church of England Cemetery in Cuddalore in 1829, but who was likewise commemorated by a cenotaph in the village of Thirukkóyilur as being 'one of the most beautiful places in the [South Arcot] district. It is among fine trees on the bank of the Ponnayár.'[154]

NOTES

1. Even for Europe, the seventeenth-century historian John Weever had been aware of the hazards to which monuments and their inscriptions were exposed. See Guthke, *Sprechende Steine*, p. 40.
2. See A. Chadha, *Ambivalent Heritage*. It is overly simplistic to contend that: 'In a postcolonial nation, the colonial masters do not have any place; they are the dead who must be removed from the sight of the living.' (p. 345) This quite ideological statement flatly denies the efforts of Christian communities in South Asia as well as of the Archaeological Survey of India to protect a number of cemeteries from decay. It furthermore has to be asked, how—for example—the Victoria Memorial in Calcutta or the Fort St. George Museum at Madras fit into this pattern and whether India can be reduced to merely a post-colonial nation.
3. IOR, 333/77, Ecclesiastical Department, G. Trevor, Chaplain at Bangalore, to the Lord Bishop of Madras, 15 December 1840. See also Cotton, *List of Inscriptions*, p. 381.
4. IOR, 333/77, Ecclesiastical Department, The Lord Bishop of Madras to the Governor in Council, 30 December 1840.
5. IOR, 333/77, Robert Clark, Secretary to Government, to the Commissioner for the Government of the Territories of the Rajah of Mysore, 11 January 1841.
6. See Chapter 3 of this book.
7. See for example, Rea, *Monumental Remains*, pp. 44f.: 'While the Portuguese and Dutch and Danish tombs still survive the power of the nationalities they present . . . English tombs have been too often flimsy in material and neglected utterly after construction.'
8. *The Times*, 14 April 1949, reader's letter of J.C. Powell-Price.
9. Consultations, 22 March 1709–10, see Penny, *Church in Madras*, vol. 1, pp. 135f.
10. Ariès, *Geschichte des Todes*, passim.

11. Consultations, 30 March 1710, see Penny, *Church in Madras*, vol. 1, pp. 136–8.
12. Consultations, 29 November 1716, see ibid., p. 138.
13. Guthke, *Sprechende Steine*, p. 215.
14. Kulke/Rothermund, *Geschichte Indiens*, pp. 283–301.
15. Penny, *Church in Madras*, vol. 1, pp. 366f.
16. Cotton, *List of Inscriptions*, p. 264.
17. Penny, *Church in Madras*, vol. 1, p. 374, vol. 2, p. 60.
18. Ibid., vol. 2, pp. 333, 336.
19. Ibid., vol. 1, p. 635.
20. Beavan, *Thirty Years in India*.
21. Rea, *Monumental Remains*, p. 44.
22. Penny, *Church in Madras*, vol. 1, p. 270.
23. Ibid., pp. 116f.
24. *Spectator*, no. 26, 30 March 1711.
25. IOR, 333/77, Ecclesiastical Department 1841.
26. IOR, 333/77, Resolution, 12 February 1841.
27. Rea, *Monumental Remains*.
28. Penny, *Church in Madras*, vol. 1, p. 251.
29. Cotton, *List of Inscriptions*, pp. 264–70.
30. See the homepage of the ASI: http://asi.nic.in. European burial sites of south India listed by the ASI are: St. Mary's Church, Madras; David Yale and Joseph Hymners tomb, Madras; Dutch Cemetery, Sadras; Schwartz' (Christ) Church, Thanjavur; Dutch Cemetery, Pulicat; Dutch Cemetery, Masulipatnam; St. Francis Church, Cochin; three European Graves, Bhatkal; Basilica Bom Jesus, Goa; Sé Cathedral, Goa; Church and Convent of St. Francis Assisi, Goa as well as a number of smaller churches/chapels in Goa.
31. IOR, R/4/114, circular of the Foreign Office, 31 March 1890.
32. IOR, R/4/114, letter of Commonwealth Relations Office to British High Commission, 8 August 1950.
33. IOR, MSS Eur. F. 146/6, Papers of Lady Lloyd, Short History of the British Monuments and Graves Section Office of the High Commissioner for the United Kingdom New Delhi, 1 January 1951.
34. The Parliamentary Debate (HANSARD), Fifth Series, volume CLXI, House of Lords, Official Report, Third Volume of Session 1948–49, London 1949, pp. 305f.
35. IOR, R/4/25, High Commission to the Office of the Deputy High Commissioner Madras, 4 August 1953. IOR, R/4/342, Sykes, British High Commission, to Gordon, Commonwealth Relations Office, 2 September 1954.

36. Parliamentary Debate (HANSARD), Fifth Series, volume CLXI, House of Lords, Official Report, Third Volume of Session 1948–49, London 1949, p. 307.
37. IOR, R/4/25, High Commission to South Indian Cemeteries Board, 25 September 1951.
38. IOR, R/4/25, letter of High Commission to B.L. Langford, Vijayawada, 13 January 1953.
39. IOR, R/4/25, letter of H. Philipps (Office of the High Commissioner for the United Kingdom, British Monuments and Graves Section) to Wallis Linnell (Honorary Secretary to the South India Cemeteries Board), 25 September 1951.
40. IOR, R/4/771, Endowments, 1925–1948.
41. See, for example, endowments for the New Cochin Cemetery, IOR, R/4/289, New Cochin Cemetery.
42. IOR, R/4/25, letter of H. Philipps (Office of the High Commissioner for the United Kingdom, British Monuments and Graves Section) to Wallis Linnell (Honorary Secretary to the South India Cemeteries Board), 25 September 1951, regarding repairs on the Kilpauk Cemetery, Madras: 'In any case, endowed graves have first claim on the endowment money, and we think that for the first two years at least there will be little or nothing over from the accrued interest to spend on repairs to walls, etc.'
43. IOR, R/4/25, letter from B.L. Langford, Church of South India, Vijayawada, to the British High Commission, 26 December 1952.
44. IOR, R/4/114, 4, Commonwealth Relation Office to High Commission, 14 May 1948.
45. IOR, R/4/114, 9, note of Bullock, Office of the High Commission, 27 October 1949.
46. IOR, R/4/6, Bullock, Office of the High Commission, to the Commonwealth Relation Office, 22 April 1949.
47. IOR, R/4/61, Chrisholm, Commonwealth Relations Office, to Bullock, British High Commission, 17 May 1949.
48. IOR, R/4/292, British High Commission to the Eastern India Cemeteries Board, 13 November 1953 and 5 March 1955.
49. See for example, IOR, R/4/25, letter from B.L. Langford, Church of South India, Vijayawada, to the British High Commission, 26 December 1952. '[The cemetery] is situated right in the heart of a busy area of the town, and local residents take every opportunity of turning their cattle into it for grazing. This can only be prevented by the re-building of the walls, large sections of which have collapsed.' Or a complaint from a Mr. Venkatachalam, Superintendent of the L.R.S. Cattle Farm, from Hosur: 'The condition of the compound wall of the cemetery of the Army Remount Depot of this

farm us in urgent need of repairs', see IOR, R/4/25, 10 July 1951; IOR, R/4/210, Municipal Councillor to CSI-Bishop, 2 November 1953 on Kilpauk Cemetery, Madras.

50. IOR, R/4/210, Rao Sahib, Municipal Councillor, to CSI-Bishop, 2 November 1953.
51. IOR, R/4/210, 6, W.O. Bullock to the British High Commission, 26 November 1955.
52. IOR, R/4/210, Minutes of the Madras Cemetery Committee, 31 July 1956.
53. IOR, R/4/25, Extract from the minutes of the meeting of the South India Cemeteries Board held on 20 November 1952.
54. Knud Heiberg records a small iron fence ('et lavt Jernrækværk') surrounding the two monuments of William Christensen Petersen and his daughter Olivia Adelaide. The fence was still there in 1972, while it had disappeared by 2002. See Handels-og Søfartsmuseet paa Kronborg, Knud Heiberg, Afskrifter af indskrifterne i Tranquebar med personalhistoriske noter, 1935, SR-bilag 1307:50: *Zion's Kirke og Kirkegaard*, p. 10 and Kryger/Gasparski, *Tranquebar*, p. 89.
55. IOR, R/4/25, South Indian Cemeteries Board to the Office of the High Commissioner, 31 August 1951.
56. Parliamentary Debate (HANSARD), Fifth Series, volume CLXI, House of Lords, Official Report, Third Volume of Session 1948–49, London 1949, p. 307.
57. IOR, R/4/210, 7, British High Commission, 5 December 1955.
58. IOR, R/4/303, note Davies, British High Commission, 4 April 1955.
59. IOR, MSS Eur. F.146/6, Papers of Lady Lloyd, Lady Lloyd to Terence Stone, Office of the British High Commissioner, 16 August 1947.
60. IOR, R/4/303, note Davies, British High Commission, 4 April 1955.
61. IOR, R/4/303, British High Commission, Memorandum, 13 October 1954; 26 November 1954; 19 January 1955; 21 May 1960.
62. In 1967, Mollie Panter-Downes reports: 'I am told later that this is the oldest graveyard in Ooty, where the first civilian settlers and soldiers and their families were buried; it must have been a short stroll away from Mr. Sullivan's elusive Stonehouse. But nothing much survives now. There are only three or four anonymous tombs—from which the inset inscriptions have been removed for some reason—sagging in ruin among the weeds and the rubbish. The cow steps daintily through a gap in the wall and begins morosely pulling at some rusty shrub beside the only tomb that can, with some difficulty, be read.' In: Mollie Panter-Downes, *Ooty Preserved: A Victorian Hill Station in India*, p. 38.
63. IOR, R/4/214, 25, High Commission to the Bishop of Madura and

Ramnad, 26 July 1963. Ibid., p. 28, Indian Ministry of External Affairs, 13 August 1963.

64. Parliamentary Debate (HANSARD), Fifth Series, volume CLXI, House of Lords, Official Report, Third Volume of Session 1948–49, London 1949, p. 308.
65. Ibid.
66. Varghese, 'Will Pulicat Make it?', *The Hindu, Business Line*, Online edn., 6 August 2001.
67. Subramanian, 'Unravelling a Dutch Past', *The Hindu*, Online edn., 14 August 2006.
68. IOR, MSS Eur. F 146/6, Papers of Lady Lloyd, Memorandum, 24 February 1947: 'European tombs and memorials in India come under 5 headings: (a) Cemeteries, regular and in use, (b) Churchyards containing graves and cenotaphs, (c) Cemeteries, closed, (d) Wayside, camp and battlefield graves and memorials, (e) War graves, 1914–1918 and 1939–45.'
69. In some instances, European burial grounds obviously had been reopened during the last two decades such as in the case of St. Stephen's Church Cemetery at Ootacamund.
70. See, in detail, Martin Krieger, *Koloniale Wohnkultur an der Koromandelküste*, pp. 409–30.
71. Banerjea, *European Calcutta*, p. 117.
72. Peters, *In steen geschreven*, p. 225. It was uncommon that interments were carried out inside the precincts of Dutch or British forts (as the remaining monuments suggest today). Only in very rare cases, individual persons seem to have been buried there.
73. Peters, *In steen geschreven*, p. 232.
74. Penny, *Church in Madras*, vol. 1, p. 261. No monument which dates back to 1651 exists in Sadras today.
75. Peters suggests that they were shifted around 1749 during the erection of the fort: Peters, *In steen geschreven*, p. 225.
76. Ibid.
77. IOR, R/4/293, List of Dutch Monuments.
78. Cemeteries partly or fully recorded: Balasore (Dinamardinga), Balasore (Farasidinga), Bimunipatnam (Walanda Bhumulu), Cochin (Dutch Cemetery), Cochin (St. Francis Church), Cuddalore, Goa (Sé Cathedral), Kotagiri (European Cemetery), Madras (St. Mary's Church/'Guava Garden'), Madras (St. Mary's Cemetery), Madras (Kilpauk Cemetery), Madurai (St. George's Cemetery), Masulipatnam (Walandapalam), Masulipatnam (Old Burial Ground), Ootacamund (St. Stephen's Cemetery), Pondicherry (Cholas Nagar, French and English Cemeteries), Parangipettai/Porto Novo

(Wannarpalaiyam), Pulicat (Binnenkerkhof), Pulicat (Buitenkerkhof), Sadras (Fort), Sadras (Protestant Cemetery), Seringapatnam, Tranquebar (Old Cemetery), Tranquebar (Zion Churchyard), Tranquebar (New Jerusalem Churchyard), Vellore, Vijayawada (Dutch ledgers from Palakollu).

79. At the onset of the twentieth century, the scattered remnants of the English burial ground at Masulipatnam were still to be seen. Penny, *Church in Madras*, vol. 1, p. 63.
80. Francis, *Vizagapatnam* (Madras District Gazetteers), pp. 227f.
81. Penny, *Church in Madras*, vol. 1, p. 65.
82. Quoted after Rea, *Monumental Remains*, p. 14.
83. IOR, G/26/12, Diary of William Puckle.
84. Penny, *Church in Madras*, vol. 2, pp. 176f.: 'The only memorial of the presence of the English merchants at the place [i.e. Masulipatnam] is the tombstone of Mr. John Rowland in a burial-ground at Engishpalem near the native town. This burial-ground was probably the English Garden where burials in the seventeenth century took place. It contains many broken stones, but only John Rowland's inscription remains legible.'
85. Quoted after Bowrey, *A Geographical Account of Countries Round the Bay of Bengal*, p. 63, ann. 1.
86. Penny, *Church in Madras*, vol. 1, p. 285.
87. Ibid., vol. 1, p. 285.
88. Francis, *South Arcot* (Madras District Gazetteers), p. 299.
89. Ratio between the number of remaining monuments and the recorded burials at St. Mary's Cemetery (Madras): 1761–70: 1:137; 1771–80: 1:117; 1781–90: 1:40; 1791–1800: 1:31; 1801–10: 1:36; 1811–20: 1:44; 1821–30: 1:62.
90. List of Burials at Madras.
91. Raychaudhuri, *Jan Company in Coromandel*, pp. 219f.
92. Furber, *Rival Empires*, p. 80.
93. See chapter 2.
94. Penny, *Church in Madras*, vol. 1, p. 319.
95. See, for example, the history of the Dutch factory at Bimunipatnam: Carmichael (ed.), *A Manual of the District of Vizagapatam in the Presidency of Madras*, pp. 273f.
96. Church of South India (ed.), *St. Mary's Church*, p. 152.
97. Penny, *Church in Madras*, vol. 1, p. 135.
98. IOR, 333/41, 26 March 1819, Madras, Ecclesiastical Consultations.
99. Despatch, 1 July 1696, 28; Consultations, 2 May 1698; see Penny, *Church in Madras*, vol. 1, p. 115.
100. Francis, *South Arcot* (Madras District Gazetteers), p. 280.

101. M. Graham, *Journal of a Residence in India*, Edinburgh, 1812, p. 141, quoted after Nilsson, *European Architecture in India*, p. 136.
102. Colvin, *Architecture and the After-Life*, p. 364.
103. Hemingway, *Trichinopoly* (Madras District Gazetteers), p. 337.
104. Penny, *Church in Madras*, vol. 1, p. 385.
105. Ibid., p. 569.
106. Vestry Proceedings, 18 January 1785; see Penny, *Church in Madras*, vol. 1, p. 403.
107. Ibid.
108. Compiled from Zions Kirkes Regnskaber. The Rd. Tranq. Courant amounted to approximately 18 per cent less than the Danish Rd.
109. Penny, *Church in Madras*, vol. 1, p. 404.
110. Ibid., p. 384.
111. IOR, P/333/40, 17 July 1818.
112. Ibid., 11 July 1818.
113. A separate Bishopric of Madras was only established in 1835; Penny, *Church in Madras*, vol. 2, p. 149.
114. See, for example, *Madras Almanac*, 1837, pp. 117–21.
115. IOR, P 333/40, 17 July 1818.
116. IOR, P/333/4, 19 January 1848, the Trustees of St. George's Cathedral to the Chief Secretary to the Government.
117. Consultations, 12 December 1800, and Vestry Proceedings, 31 December 1800; see Penny, *Church in Madras*, vol. 1, p. 406.
118. *Madras Almanac*, 1837, p. 121.
119. Boswell, *A Manual of the Nellore District in the Presidency of Madras*, p. 693.
120. Despatch, 2 July 1841, 18, Eccl., see Penny, *Church in Madras*, vol. 2, p.118.
121. Ibid.
122. Kryger and Gasparski, *Tranquebar*, pp. 145–7.
123. See Zions Kirkebog, 11 December 1798: 'Underofficeer Schmutz paa den gamle Kirkegaard tæt til Volden i Krogen mod Vest, da han i Vildelse formodes at have hængt sig.' Ibid., 17 December 1798: 'En Konstabel navnlig A. Funke paa den gamle Kirkegaard paa samme Plads som ovenførte, da han ligeledes havde hængt sig selv, men efter formodning i Vildelse'.
124. Wilkinson, *Two Monsoons*, p. 188.
125. Tranquebar, Zions Kirkebog, 22 September 1798.
126. Penny, *Church in Madras*, p. 180.
127. Francis, *Nilgiris*, p. 338.

128. Penny, *Church in Madras*, vol. 2, p. 71.
129. Ibid., vol. 1, pp. 602f.
130. Wilkinson, *Two Monsoons*, p. 143.
131. Deloche, *Senji* (*Gingee*), pp. 127, 162.
132. Stephen, *Portuguese in the Tamil Coast*, p. 233. Peters, *In steen geschreven*, p. 199.
133. Ariès, *Geschichte des Todes*.
134. Ibid., p. 64.
135. Ibid., pp. 64f.
136. Ibid., p. 66.
137. Penny, *Church in Madras*, vol. 1, pp. 253f.
138. Ibid., p. 86.
139. A very small number of Englishmen and Germans is likewise attributed to the 'Dutch'-curve.
140. Houlbrooke, *Death, Religion and the Family in England*, p. 334.
141. Ibid.
142. IOR, Vestry Minutes, 21 June 1777, see Penny, *Church in Madras*, vol. 1, pp. 367f.
143. Ibid., p. 368.
144. IOR, Vestry Minutes, 22 November 1784, see ibid., p. 368.
145. Ibid., p. 395f.
146. Ibid., p. 395.
147. Ibid., p. 599.
148. Ibid., p. 610.
149. Ibid., p. 289.
150. Ibid., vol. 2, p. 129.
151. Gøbel, *Jens Mortensen Sveigaards ostindiske rejsebeskrivelse*, p. 90.
152. IOR, L/AG/34/29/222, Madras Wills 1822/23, George Boyd, 10 November 1818.
153. Penny, *Church in Madras*, vol. 1, p. 144.
154. Francis, *South Arcot*, pp. 377f.

CHAPTER 3

The Monuments

COMMISSIONING AND ERECTION OF MONUMENTS

Investigating death merely against the backdrop of personal or collective mourning and self-perception seems to be too restrictive. Death generated business and constituted a source of income for churches, artisans and undertakers. Stones had to be carved and transported, funerals had to be organized, and space for the deceased had to be procured within the burial grounds. While the funeral of the poorer Europeans was usually carried out in the simplest and cheapest manner, the interment of a wealthy person or a person of repute proved to be a most expensive affair. Who were the people behind this business? Who carved the inscriptions on the numerous European monuments in south India, who organized the funeral services? Sources on this subject are very limited, especially for the seventeenth and eighteenth centuries. A rough picture can nevertheless be drawn.

As early as the seventeenth century, most of the characteristic Dutch and English ledgers of the colonial burial grounds were obviously produced in India itself. The stone slabs from the seventeenth- and eighteenth-century Indian east coast were usually carved from hard hornblende (Dutch: *arduinsteen*). This raw material—traditionally also used for the creation of many Hindu sculptures—obviously came down from the hills of the Eastern Ghats.[1] Hornblende is notably to be found on several hill tracts of the hinterland of the southern east coast such as in the Thiruchirapalli and the Chingleput district or in the hills around Vishakhapatnam.[2] The relative proximity of these regions to the coast might have facilitated the transport of the raw stone blocks to the European trading settlements over land and along the coasts.

Since the mid-seventeenth century, the Dutch trading settlement Sadras, south of today's Madras, served as a major centre for carving these stones and as an outlet for exporting them to other regions around the Indian Ocean. A number of villages surrounding the Dutch settlement obviously had specialized in this business.[3] In these villages, not only tomb monuments, but also other stone artefacts such as portals or parts of pediments were produced as per European taste and exported to other parts of the Coromandel coast, Ceylon, Batavia or Malacca.[4] However, it remains uncertain, whether or not the slabs were merely the product of local Hindu sculptors, or if European specialists were responsible for carving the epitaphs and coats-of-arms. Alexander Rea contends, that the slabs 'have been partly cut by native workman, but under the direction of trained European stone carvers'.[5] He derives this idea from his observation, that the ornamental decoration of the slabs had Indian characteristics, while inscriptions and coat-of-arms proved to be European—an issue which will be discussed in detail in heading 'Inscriptions' of this chapter.[6]

In many instances, the border decorations on the stone slabs from Sadras, Pulicat, Nagapattinam and Masulipatnam exhibit similar features, and sometimes they seem to be virtually identical. However, other patterns are only to be found in individual places, so that it cannot be contended that every Dutch slab in Coromandel was carved in the workshops of Sadras or was influenced by them in style. In many instances, the size of the stone slabs was standardized, which supports the hypothesis of trading from Sadras to other places in Coromandel. Ledgers relating to slabs of the size 2.49–2.67 m × 1.24–1.35 m constituted the largest share of those to be found along Coromandel.[7] In some instances, apparently semi-finished stone slabs, bearing only border decoration but without any inscription, were exported to places such as Masulipatnam, where two of them are still to be found (Plate 13). Stone slabs were obviously not transported from Sadras to the Malabar Coast, where other sorts of stone and decoration and other sizes of the slabs were in use, as an investigation of the Dutch stone slabs in St. Francis Church of Cochin reveals.[8]

A number of south Indian stone slabs from Sadras obviously

also found its way to Dutch burial grounds in South-East Asia, notably to Malacca, as identical border decorations suggest.[9]

The early English monuments in Coromandel resemble the Dutch slabs, but they are, however, not identical in decoration and shape. It may be suggested—even if it cannot be verified from the sources—that a number of workshops also existed around the settlements of the English East India Company. According to the material evidence on the English burial grounds, such workshops characterized by a more sophisticated output might have been established only at the onset of the eighteenth century.[10] Against this backdrop, a tight trading connection must have been established between Coromandel and Bengal—even if it cannot be reconstructed into which direction the ledgers were transported or if just the patterns diffused. A number of early eighteenth-century slabs from St. John's Church at Calcutta shows exactly the same features of border decoration as the ledgers from St. Mary's cemetery at Madras of the same time.[11]

While the production of the monuments can only roughly be reconstructed for the seventeenth and eighteenth centuries, it becomes obvious, that the East India Companies—especially the English East India Company—played a decisive function in commissioning them. The local company authorities usually applied to their respective governments in India or to their headquarters in Europe for sponsoring such monuments, which was sanctioned in many cases. For example, in 1682 it was ordered by the English East India Company to create a monument for the deceased manager of the English factory in Masulipatnam, Maurice Wynn. The Company headquarters in London developed a detailed design for the monument in regards to the amount to be spent on this issue and the contents of the epitaph.[12] A century later, this practice was still in use, such as in the case of the prominent Lieut. Colonel Moorhouse (see above). It was decided, 'that his remains [. . .] be publicly interred in the Church of Fort St. George, at the Company's expense and a marble tablet fixed over his grave with a suitable inscription in commemoration of his merits.'[13] A representative monument was created by Charles Peart, indeed symbolizing Britannia seated on a lion recognizing a medallion head of the deceased.[14] Next to the East India Company, missionary societies likewise commissioned monuments for a small number of distinguished promoters of the Gospel from the eighteenth century onwards.[15]

At the same time, it became common practice to raise private capital for representative monuments, when financial support was denied by the Company or when the deceased had not been employed in the Company's service. After the death of a member of the European community, it thus became common to launch a subscription for erecting a tomb monument, which especially features the nineteenth century. The more money could be collected, the more representative the monument would become—even at the risk of overstressing the financial resources of some of the bereaved.[16] It seems likely that most subscriptions were launched by family members, friends or the soldiers' comrades, as many of the inscriptions suggest. For example, the epitaph commemorating the missionary and minister Johann Peter Rottler inside St. Matthias' Church in Vepery (Madras) was financed by a subscription from the local European and Tamil Christians.[17]

The latter half of the eighteenth and the beginning of the nineteenth century brought about increasing commercial and social activities of private European entrepreneurs especially under British colours. Many branches formerly monopolized by the Company were now handed over to private hands—the famous British Agency Houses being a prominent example.[18] The funeral-business likewise emerged as a distinct sector of the local economy and—from the beginning of the nineteenth century—as a mere private enterprise. A matching trend was established in Bengal, and Calcutta in particular. The new profession of the undertaker now commercialized and professionalized the business of death. The undertaker not only commissioned the monuments according to the wishes of his customers, but he also arranged for the funeral service and the burial in the cemetery.

During the eighteenth century, the duties of the undertaker in British Madras still had been in the hands of the Company. They were fulfilled by one junior civil servant, who received a monthly salary of 25 pagodas for his efforts. After the last civil servant to be entrusted with this office had resigned at the end of that century, the office was handed over to the Chaplains of St. Mary's Church, whose allowances were increased simultaneously.[19] However, by 1805, in the course of the dissolution of the Vestry, the profession of undertaker was entirely handed over to private enterprise.[20] The commencement of private undertaking in Madras proved to occur quite late in comparison to British Bengal, where the first private entrepreneurs appear during the 1780s.[21]

The nineteenth century witnessed an enormous increase of the number of private undertakers and sculptors and a significant differentiation in the business. Generally, three types of this enterprise can be distinguished: one only being engaged in the undertaker's profession, another combining the profession of undertaker and sculptor and the third merely concentrating on sculpturing and architecture, sometimes in combination with masonry or architectural work outside the cemeteries.[22] Most of the entrepreneurs were of European origin, however, in a few instances also Indian/Tamil names are recorded; and European undertakers drew on the services of Indian sculptors as well, such as in the case of Fenn & Co. in Madras.[23]

Most of the smaller south Indian workshops were presumably active on a local or regional level. And many smaller European settlements did not have their own sculptor, or at least none is recorded. Only Madras, Thiruchirapalli (Trichinopoly) and Bangalore served as major outlets for monuments and inscription-plaques and dominated the market of entire south India during the nineteenth and twentieth centuries. A differentiation between the construction of a monument—made of bricks by local stone-masons[24]—and sophisticated, but lighter inscription plaques facilitated trading of these plaques on a larger scale even into the hinterland. Even large and tremendously heavy monuments were transported in pieces. Nevertheless, international operations of south Indian undertakers and sculptors could not be identified—unlike the entrepreneurs of Calcutta, who exported inscription plaques to other countries around the Indian Ocean such as to British Singapore or Malacca.[25]

The southern Coromandel Coast was furnished with inscription-plaques both from Madras and Thiruchirapalli, while places farther inland and the hill stations were supplied by Madras, Thiruchirapalli and Bangalore (Plate 14). The northern Coromandel Coast, on the other hand, was a domain jointly shared by Madras and Calcutta. While an almost equal number of inscriptions from Calcutta and Madras is to be found in the nineteenth- and twentieth-century British cemetery at Waltair, more inscriptions from Madras are to be found on the Mors Janua Vitae Cemetery of nearby Vizagapatnam.[26] On the other hand, sculptors from Calcutta predominate in the Flagstaff Cemetery of Bimunipatnam some 30 km further north.[27]

Ootacamund proves to be another example, where a geographical division of labour applied (see Figure 25). Until 1844, plaques in Ootacamund were almost exclusively supplied from Madras and Thiruchirapalli with minor supplies from Calcutta and London. The latter half of the nineteenth century proved to be more diversified. Now Bangalore emerged as the third major supplier of plaques and soon superseded Madras and Thiruchirapalli. It becomes obvious, that the rise of Bangalore's trading in inscription-plaques was carried out at Tiruchirapalli's expense. An increasing importance of inscription-plaques from Bangalore in Ootacamund from the 1840s corresponds to the completion of the Sigur Ghat-road connecting Ootacamund with Mysore and further northwards with Bangalore in 1838. The new road replaced an old track which

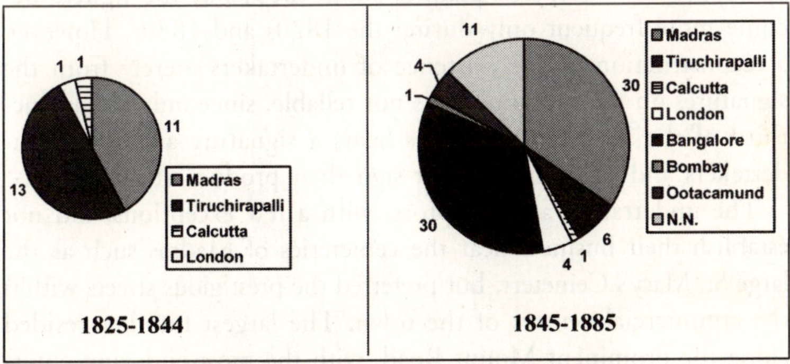

Figure 25: Origin of inscription-plaques at St. Stephen's Cemetery, Ootacamund

was dangerous even for those travelling by foot, while the new one was comfortably viable for bullock carts. This new facility enormously enhanced passenger traffic and trade between the plains and the Nilgiris, and even the transport of goods from Madras was now largely diverted from the Coimbatore-Coonoor road to this new road via Bangalore.[28] Facing the sometimes tremendous weight of stone slabs to be transported uphill on bullock-carts—even very ordinary slabs could weigh more than half a ton,[29] the condition of transport-routes must have been decisive. We may thus well presume that the improvement of infrastructure enhanced an increasing influx of inscription-plaques and ledges from Bangalore to Ootacamund.

When investigating the profession of the undertaker in colonial south India, Madras as the major colonial emporium serves as the best example. However, unlike Calcutta, where the voluminous diary of Richard Blechynden unveils the contemporary discourses on sepulchral architecture and undertaking between 1791 and 1822,[30] records prove to be limited even here. The signatures on the monuments themselves, the mentioning of undertakers in the commercial lists of the 'Madras Almanac' as well as the recorded correspondence of the Ecclesiastical Department of Madras serve as the most important sources on this issue, while private records from the undertakers themselves could not be found.

First, private undertakers in Madras can be gleaned from the signatures of inscription-plaques since 1809, but the figures become more frequent only during the 1820s and 1830s. However, a reconstruction of the existence of undertakers merely from the signatures on the monuments is not reliable, since only about one-third of the inscription-plaques bears a signature and many undertakers and sculptors did not sign their produce at all.

The undertakers and sculptors, with a few exceptions, did not establish their business near the cemeteries of Madras such as the large St. Mary's Cemetery, but preferred the prestigious streets within the commercial centres of the town. The largest number resided along the prominent Mount Road, with the most enduring enterprises of the Ostheider and the Law family.[31] During the nineteenth century, Mount Road housed not only the leading south

Indian newspapers, but also a number of prominent showrooms and workshops, like that of the well-known coach-builder A.M. Simpson, the prominent jeweller Peter Orr or R. Maclure's pharmacy, famous for its 'Maclure's Soda Water'.[32] A second popular place was the commercial and residential quarters north and north-west of Fort St. George, in particular George Town, Egmore, Vepery and Purasawalkam. It was Popham's Broadway (today's Prakasam Road) in George Town, the main commercial road of nineteenth-century Madras, which likewise housed several undertakers and sculptors, including Elizabeth (house no. 173) and Thomas (house no. 175) De Sena.[33] In Vepery and Purasawalkam, the undertaker's business mainly focused on the Vepery High Road,[34] Poonamallee Road[35] and Kennett's Road near St. Andrew's Kirk.[36] Localizing the shops of undertakers and sculptors in nineteenth-century Madras leaves the impression that they were perceived as an integral part of the local economy and were thus situated in the commercial centre of the town with its customers and abundant social life and not near the remote cemeteries.

Figure 26 illustrates the period of existence of the various undertakers and sculptors in Madras as recorded in the *Madras*

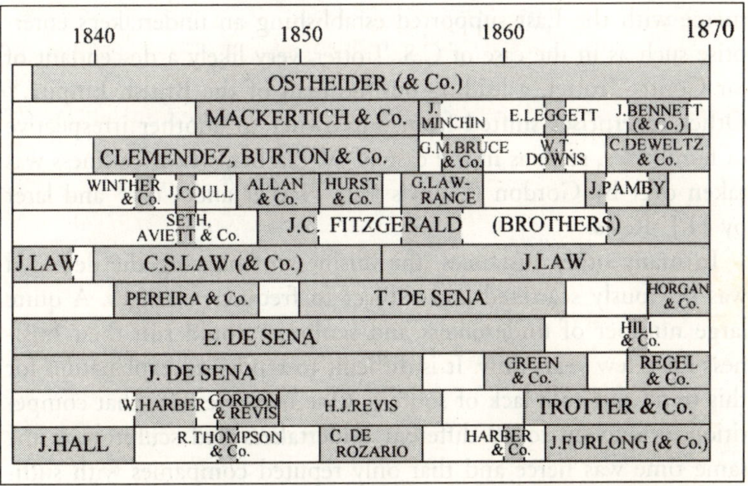

Figure 26: Sculptors and undertakers in Madras, 1835–70. (Source: *Madras Almanac and Compendium*)

Almanac and Compendium. With the exception of C.S. Trotter, whose enterprise is not recorded between the 1830s and the 1850s, and Fenn & Co., already founded in 1854, the Almanac proves to be a reliable source when compared with the signatures on the surviving monuments. An impressive number of 37 individual companies is recorded for the period between 1835 and 1870. Eight more enterprises can be gleaned from the inscriptions for the period between 1809 and 1834.

Records, however, reveal that only a small number of enterprises such as Ostheider, Mackertich, Clemendez, Burton & Co., Trotter & Co., the Law family as well as the De Sena family survived at least for one decade. Ostheider proved to emerge as the most enduring company with activities carried out well into the twentieth century. Some companies changed hands from the husband to the wife or between the generations such as in the case of the Law or the De Sena family. Edward De Sena, for example, must have started his business around 1820, as the surviving signatures on St. Mary's cemetery reveal. He was succeeded by John and Elizabeth De Sena, who most likely were his children. In 1850, Thomas De Sena (Elizabeth's son?) launched his own enterprise next to Elizabeth's workshop. It seems likely that a family's general expertise in commerce with the East supported establishing an undertaker's enterprise such as in the case of C.S. Trotter, very likely a descendant of Sir Coutts Trotter, a leading businessman of the British Empire.[37] Other enterprises shifted from one owner to another irrespective of family ties, such as in the case of W. Harber, whose business was taken over by Gordon & Revis (late Harber and Co.)[38] and later by H.J. Revis.

In many other instances, the business of burying the deceased was obviously scattered and subject to frequent changes. A quite large number of undertakers and sculptors could run their business for a few years only. It is difficult to render an explanation for this trend due to a lack of sources. One may presume that competition among up to 10 different undertakers and sculptors at the same time was fierce and that only reputed companies with sufficient capital could sustain such a competition (Plate 15).

The funeral business was not merely a male enterprise, as sources reveal. Four sculptresses are recorded for Madras, such as a certain Mrs. Furlong, Frances Godfrey, Charlotte Sarah Law and the already mentioned Elizabeth De Sena, a member of the De Sena sculptor family from Madras.

Competition obviously stimulated the sculptors and undertakers making use of the printed media to offer their services. Several companies regularly published their advertisements in the *Madras Almanac and Compendium*. These advertisements unveil a multitude of activities apart from producing inscription-plaques and preparing funerals, such as trading in 'Miscellaneous Goods' or house building. Exhumations were also carried out by them, but were not mentioned in the advertisements.[39] The information that the undertakers' produce was being transported to other places within India deserves special attention against the backdrop of our observation on the broad range of some undertaker's activities. Announcements such as 'Up-country Orders Attended with Great Care' or 'Executed and Packed and Forwarded to any Part of India' informed the customers about this special service, which obviously constituted a major source of income to many enterprises. J. Leese's & Cos.' notice 'By appointment to the "General Hospital"', for instance, unveils the increasing institutionalization of dying from the end of the nineteenth century. At the same time, the advertisements offer an insight into specialization regarding stone work. While Trotter especially mentions the polishing of granite tombs, Law obviously wanted to highlight his expertise in marbles.

Given the competition among quite a large number of sculptors and undertakers in south India, only very few inscription-plaques were imported from Europe during the nineteenth century. This observation supports the picture that India served as an exporter of inscriptions-plaques rather than as an importer. Most of the few imported inscription-plaques came from London firms such as E.M. Lander at Kensal Green (Bimunipatnam), Cox Buckley & Co. (Tranquebar)—also famed for its stained glass windows—, Barker & Son (Ootacamund) or Burke (Ootacamund), mainly during the latter half of the nineteenth century.[40] One single monument at Kotagiri was manufactured by McGlasman at Edinburgh.[41] Marble and brass epitaphs by T. Goffin from London survive till today in Trinity Church, Bangalore. Imports from Europe were usually arranged through south Indian agency houses such as Messrs. Arbuthnot and Co. in Bentinck's Building on North Beach in Madras—'the Premier Mercantile Firm of South India'.[42] Arbuthnot and Co. obviously cooperated with its offshoot, Messrs. Arbuthnot, Latham and Co., in London.[43]

There is almost no evidence about of the fate of the British undertakers after Indian Independence in 1947. We may well presume that most of them abandoned their business and returned to Great Britain during the 1940s such as in the case of the owner of P. Swaries & Co. from Calcutta, who sold his enterprise and returned to Europe.[44] A few others had transferred their business over into Indian hands in good time, like Fenn & Co. in Madras. The last British owner, John Fenn, had handed over his enterprise to Vembuli Nayakar, a former contractor, as early as in 1892. Later, Fenn & Co. gained prominence for having introduced the first motorized hearse in Madras, in 1931.[45] The company obviously represents the only surviving undertaker of Madras if not of entire south India from the colonial period still existing today.[46]

ARCHITECTURE AND DECORATION

The most important source for studying death and burial culture in colonial south India are the innumerable surviving monuments. They not only render insight into personal affection and a very individual reception of death, but also into collective identities. Furthermore, they are a significant indicator of political and mercantile strength and of cultural exchange, which not only took place between Europe and India, but also between the European settlements in north India and the south. From the onset of the Portuguese expansion in Asia, one notices an evolution of European funerary architecture on the subcontinent of almost half a millennium. Tremendous changes in architecture, decoration and the choice of raw material took place during this time, whilst both European and local Indian impacts can be perceived.[47] However, the monuments do not bear witness to the burial culture of the entire colonial population, especially during the earlier periods of the European expansion to Asia, as only the rich, powerful or lucky were commemorated by an enduring monument. Most of the European sailors or privates had to contend with a wooden cross or no memorial at all. Only from the second half of the nineteenth century do the monuments offer a more or less representative survey of all social classes.

The dilapidated condition of most burial grounds today imposes tremendous problems to gain a representative picture of the material evidence. Seventeenth- and eighteenth-century horizontal ledgers generally prove to be more enduring than the brittle masonry work of vertical monuments of the same period. The ledgers of Coromandel are generally much better preserved than those from Malabar due to the use of a different kind of stone. Completely undisturbed cemeteries are rare in south India. For example, the 'Binnenkerkhof' of formerly Dutch Pulicat or the cemetery of St. Stephen's Church at Ootacamund seem to be more or less intact. In other instances it is obvious that monuments had been shifted from their original position to other places. This in particular applies to the Dutch monuments at Masulipatnam and of Palakollu, the latter can now be seen in the park of the Victoria Jubilee Museum in Vijayawada. In other cases it cannot clearly be decided, if monuments still retain their original position or not such as in the case of Dutch Sadras.[48] Any generalization on the architectural heritage must therefore be carried out with caution.

Four stylistic trends of European funerary architecture in south India can be distinguished:

1. the Portuguese period dominated by ledgers and intra-mural burials (*c.* 1500–1650),
2. the period of the northwest European trading companies dominated by ledgers and early vertical monuments (*c.* 1650–1770),
3. the Neo-classical period (*c.* 1770–1860), and
4. the period of the Gothic revival and modern styles (from *c.* 1860).

The different styles do not constitute a clear chronological sequence, since they are chronologically overlapping. They transpire from very specific architectural features, decoration, techniques and choice of material.

The Portuguese Period

The Indo–Portuguese sepulchral architecture has its roots in a European, medieval perception of death and resurrection. Stone slabs embedded horizontally into the floors of churches or on the grounds of cemeteries symbolize the transience of the corpse and its return to earth until resurrection and reunification with the soul.[49] They likewise serve as an expression of humbleness of the deceased when facing God. Such monuments, according to Karl Borromäus 'non excedens pavimentum'[50] (not exceeding the pavement), constituted the only officially accepted type of tomb, which complied with the policy of the Roman Catholic 'Counter-Reformation' of the sixteenth and early seventeenth century. This idea was, however, never fully realized and was counterpoised by the monumental and representative vertical Renaissance funerary monuments of the Christian Mediterranean and beyond.[51]

Another feature of such traditional perception of death was interments inside the churches. It expressed the believers' desire to be buried as close as possible to the tombs of saints, relics or at least the altarpiece. A visible ledger inside the church might have attracted the living to remember the deceased in their prayers and to stimulate intersession—a wish, which could virtually be highlighted by the inscriptions of the monuments. For example, the inscription commemorating Joãnna da Cruz (d. 1618) at Mylapore in Coromandel asks the passerby to recite one 'Kyrie Elaison' and an 'Ave Maria' for the deceased.[52] Among Reformed communities, an intra-mural burial indicated the social reputation of the deceased rather than served any religious purpose. Similar to vertical monuments, burials inside churches nevertheless had been contested from early medieval times, but they could never entirely be banned in Europe prior to the Napoleonic period (see above). Especially during the sixteenth and seventeenth centuries, the clerical ban was frequently repeated and it was often contended that 'in ecclesia vero nulli deinceps sepeliatur'[53]—a clear indicator of the fact that it virtually could never be contained. Portuguese India is especially characterized by intra-mural interments.

Today, most Portuguese funerary monuments survive in the

churches or church ruins of the West coast, notably in Goa and Cochin. Only a small number of ledgers can be spotted in the former Portuguese settlements in Coromandel, which had only loosely been integrated into the *Estado da India*. It is almost impossible to locate Portuguese burial grounds outside churches, since most of them obviously had been destroyed and perished in the course of time. A large number of Portuguese ledgers was abused as building material for doorsteps or as platforms of wells such as in the case of Cochin,[54] while a number of tombs from Portuguese Mylapore found its way to the local Kapaleeswarar temple.[55] For want of material evidence, historical place names sometimes serve as a useful complement. In formerly Danish Tranquebar and Dutch Pulicat, two burial places till today bear the name 'Portuguese Cemetery', while the term 'Portuguese' often renders a synonym for the entire Roman Catholic Indo–European community. The Portuguese cemetery of Pulicat later became the Dutch 'Buitenkerkhof'.[56]

The Church of St. Francis of Assisi of Old Goa, founded after 1517, serves as an excellent example of illustrating the shapes and decoration of Portuguese stone slabs (Plate 16). The floor of the building is entirely covered by about 250 brown and dark grey stone-ledgers. They leave the impression that virtually every square-inch was utilized for burials—a vivid indicator of the wide acceptance of intra-mural burials among the Portuguese in India. The ledgers mainly commemorate Portuguese nobles or laymen. While the oldest derive from the 1520s, most of them had been created during the latter half of the sixteenth and the first half of the seventeenth century. However, a substantial number does not bear any date.

Three types of ledgers are to be distinguished: The first type is from the first half of the sixteenth century and does not possess any decoration. Another type is decorated with simple border lines, in many cases featuring double- or triple-bows at the head of the ledger. These line decorations have proved to be tremendously enduring and are to be found on the ledgers from the mid-sixteenth to the mid-seventeenth century onwards in Goa (but not at St.

Francis Church in Cochin). Only a smaller number (constituting the third type) is decorated with coats of arms of the respective families and scrollwork—a feature chiefly characterizing the monuments created after the 1630s. The inscriptions on all types are generally executed in low relief with capital Roman letters and Arabic numerals, while only the oldest monuments bear Gothic characters.

Two places of Roman Catholic worship in south India combined interments with pilgrimage. The older one was the Portuguese Church above the supposed relics of St. Thomas at Mylapore in Coromandel (today within the precincts of modern Madras/Chennai). A Nestorian chapel had already existed during the medieval period. In 1524, the Portuguese constructed a new Roman Catholic church next to this building. At the onset of the seventeenth century, the relics were removed from their original site close to the beach further inlands, where another church was erected.[57] These buildings obviously not only served as places of worship and pilgrimage but also of interments, as a number of surviving Portuguese stone slabs in the adjoining cathedral-museum suggests.

A quite exceptional edifice is the monument displaying the remains of the Portuguese missionary Francis Xavier (1506–52) at Bom San Jesus in Goa, which takes up the outstanding Medieval and Early Modern tradition of Iberian funerary architecture (Plate 17). The Basque Jesuit missionary had been a close associate of Ignatius of Loyola, the founder of the Jesuit order. After having sojourned in Venice and Rome, he went out for a missionary enterprise to the East. His major areas of work were in Goa, Ceylon, Malacca and Japan. He died en route to China from Goa in 1552, whereupon his body was packed with lime inside a wooden coffin to prevent the decay of the corpse. During the following centuries, Xavier's earthly remains emerged as a source of relics, starting in 1614, with one forearm to be cut-off on the orders of Pope Paul V. Xavier's tremendous importance as the founder of the Jesuit mission in the East and his attraction as a goal for pilgrimage resulted in the creation of a magnificent monument which proves to be quite unique for early modern India. A silver sarcophagus was created by

Goan silversmiths between approx. 1635 and 1641 after the designs of the Italian Jesuit Marcello Mastrilli. It was especially the annual exposure of St. Xavier's body inside this sarcophagus, which attracted pilgrims during the seventeenth century. Thomas Bowrey, the famous seventeenth-century English merchant, was one of the visitors to see this place during the 1670s:

> We paid a Visit to the *Domo of Bon Jesu*, the Church an admirable Piece, the Repository of St. *Xaverius*, the *Indian* Apostle, where is a famous Tomb in Honour of him, who first spread the Gospel as far as *China*, and sealed it with his Martyrdom, near two hundred years ago, leaving his Body a Miracolous Relick of his better part, it still retaining its vivid Colour and Freshness, and therefore exposed once a year to publick view, on the Vespers of his Festival.[58]

Some decades after Bowrey's visit, the sarcophagus was finally surmounted by a marble pedestal monument. The latter was commissioned by Cosimo III, Grand Duke of Tuskany, and created by Giovanni Battista Foggini in Florence (1652–1737). After the monument had been displayed at Florence for two years, it was taken apart and transported to Goa to be re-erected in the Church of Bom Jesus in 1697.[59] Even if the monument of Francis Xavier proves to be a single and outstanding piece of art, it renders an eminent example of the transfer of style and architecture from the European Mediterranean to South Asia during the seventeenth century.

The Period of the Northwest European Trading Companies

While the Portuguese had dominated the sixteenth-century European trade in the Indian Ocean, they were soon superseded by the Dutch and later by the English. The Dutch East India Company (VOC) was a modern joint stock company, and much more capital could be accrued compared to the chiefly royal Portuguese enterprise in the East. The Dutch succeeded in ousting the Portuguese from their most vital positions in south India until the 1660s, while only San Thomé/Mylapore (until 1749), Goa (until 1961) and some minor possessions in the northwest of India remained in Portuguese hands. The official religious denomination within the United Netherlands and their overseas possessions was reformed Calvinism, albeit a large number of Netherlanders still retained their traditional Roman Catholic faith during the seventeenth and eighteenth centuries.[60] The tremendous wealth in the Dutch Republic brought about flourishing arts and architecture, which gradually spread across the north and the Baltic Seas and likewise influenced artistic produce in the overseas world. Private households inside the Dutch settlements along the coasts of the Indian Ocean as well as Company authorities and local rulers commissioned art objects from the Netherlands, and paintings were a sought-after present for the indigenous elites as well. The probate inventories of the Netherlanders in Asia regularly mention Dutch paintings. Furthermore, Dutch painters and artists served in the East not only within the settlements of the VOC but also for indigenous rulers.[61] We may thus contend that a significant transfer of artistic knowledge and style must have occurred between the Netherlands and the Indian Ocean region, especially during the seventeenth century, which also transpires from the funerary architecture in south India.[62]

During the seventeenth century, the English East India Company could by no means compete with the Dutch VOC. While the VOC drew on the tremendous richness of the Indonesian spice trade, the English were mainly confined to the Indian subcontinent. This position proved to be of advantage only from the onset of the eighteenth century with an increasing trading in Indian textiles to Europe. At the same time, the EIC struggled with the economical repercussions of the Civil War and its aftermath. Furthermore, artistic transfers between England and India hardly took place to the same extent as during the latter half of the eighteenth century.[64]

Due to the devastations of the Seven Years' War, not much material evidence is left from the early English burial grounds in the south. The remaining ledgers from the old Guava Garden near Fort St. George prove to be the only source of any significance. However, the remaining English and Dutch material evidence suggests that the stone ledger was the dominating type of funerary monument in the English and Dutch possessions in south India prior to the 1780s. This preference might have derived from Europe itself, where intra-mural interment was widely accepted during the Early Modern period—a tradition, which favoured the use of ledgers. While the Reformation had abandoned the religious necessity of being buried inside the churches, worldly reasons of social representation remained and gave rise to an enormous number of burials inside churches as illustrated, for example, by a number of Dutch Early Modern paintings and prints.[64]

The numerous surviving stone slabs in the churches of Amsterdam, Haarlem, Groningen and other places bear witness to the wide acceptance of intra-mural burials in the Netherlands. Between 1410 and 1865, for example, about 10,000 people were buried inside the Nieuwe Kerk in Amsterdam, while only a small share of them was commemorated by a ledger.[65] Some burials were carried out still during the nineteenth century, even if the French occupants had banned intra-mural interments by 1810, which was confirmed again in 1829.[66] Most ledgers inside the churches of the Netherlands are plain and do not bear any decoration, but only render name or abstract symbols and a number. Only very few monuments with coats of arms and decorated by (Renaissance) scrollwork are to be discovered, while border decorations are generally missing.

Similar to Portugal, the ledger was also transferred into the colonial world, albeit in an entirely different local context and in a different appearance. Instead of church floors, Dutch ledgers in India were mainly situated outside at cemeteries on the ground or on low foundations, as well as on tombs. They could also be affixed to vertical monuments as for instance to the obelisk commemorating Adriana Catharina Pla and Adriana Appels on the 'Karikop' of Nagapattinam, from the first half of the eighteenth century. Apart from the prevailing interment outside churches in India, it is the entirely different decoration and opulent inscriptions which render the Dutch ledgers in India a unique example for European funerary sculpture. This observation gives rise to the assumption that entirely different traditions of burial architecture emerged in the Netherlandish colonial world in the East during the seventeenth century than at home.

Two artistic schools developed within the possessions of the VOC in south India: one (with only a small number of surviving examples) drew on the Indo–Portuguese tradition and brought about intra-mural interments, but also rather simple ledgers resembling the Portuguese monuments in Goa or Cochin. This school is confined to the Malabar Coast as it transpires from the Dutch ledgers in St. Francis Church at Cochin. With only a few exceptions, they are characterized by a very coarse sculpturing without border decorations. The characters are hardly sophisticated, while the coats-of-arms usually prove to be the only decoration of the ledgers.

A second, somewhat broader school developed along the east coast with interments on burial grounds and highly sophisticated and standardized products, which dispersed between Coromandel and South-East Asia, notably to Malacca and Batavia. This development indicates a striking professionalization of artistic produce at the Coromandel Coast, which characterized the century between about 1650 and 1750 (Plate 18). The ledgers now generally boost standardized sizes,[67] highly sophisticated, typographic letters, a border decoration and coats-of-arms. This highly developed art form ceased during the latter half of the eighteenth century—a period, which is generally regarded as a time of decay of Dutch India trade due to an increasing competition by private English intra-Asiatic trade and hostilities between the VOC and the French in Coromandel.[68] Artistic decay becomes apparent with a decline of typographic engraving of letters, the missing of border decorations as well as the withdrawal of standardized sizes of ledgers.

Against this backdrop, an investigation of the decorations—notably of heraldry, border decoration and death-symbolism—seems to be rewarding. A striking feature of the Netherlandish seventeenth-century stone slabs are the elaborate coats-of-arms. The remaining ledgers from the Dutch cemeteries at Pulicat unveil the fact that this form of decoration increasingly gained importance during the 1650s and 1660s, while virtually every monument was decorated with such symbols between 1677 and 1723. Only from the 1720s, a significant number of ledgers without coats-of-arms are to be found again.

What inspired the Dutch in India as well as in South-East Asia, in particular, to attach importance to such symbols during the latter half of the seventeenth and the first decades of the eighteenth century? If the mother country did not generate this tradition to such an extent, the answer might be found on the shores of the Indian Ocean itself. We may presume that this development was furthered by an advanced know-how and a tremendous diversification and professionalism of Indo–European sculpturing, which took place during the latter half of the seventeenth century.[69] Furthermore, we have to take into account, that it is chiefly the memorials commemorating members of the colonial elite which survive in Coromandel today, while the churches of the mother country boost an even larger number of middle-class burials instead. This impression of coats-of-arms being mainly favoured by the elites is also supported by the remaining monuments from the 'Pettah Cemetery' at Colombo. This burial ground was mainly reserved for private merchants and lower ranks of the Company personnel, and the monuments do not display coats-of-arms.[70]

The engravings on the ledgers either render historical family symbols or are just fantasy emblems, which in many cases refer to the name of the deceased itself: The symbol on the tomb of the family Visser at Nagapattinam is, for instance, a fish, while the family Pfeiffer (piper) from Porto Novo is commemorated by a musician.[71] Two tremendously interesting, individual coats-of-arms are to be found on the monuments commemorating Abraham and Louis Mendis from the Binnenkerkhof at Pulicat. The Portuguese free merchant Abraham Mendis died in 1684 and was buried on the Binnenkerkhof of Pulicat. Instead of an ordinary coat-of-arms, his ledger bears a round emblem showing a fortress with four bastions (Plate 19). We recognize a typical European fortified trading settlement which, for example, resembles the still-existing Danish fortress Dansborg at Tranquebar some 270 km south of Pulicat.[72] At the bottom of the emblem, creepers are to be found, in the background on the right bushes, and on the left an ensemble of huts. A comparison of the engraving with Schouten's description of Pulicat from 1662 renders striking similarities:

> The fort of Gueldres [i.e. Fort Geldria at Pulicat] . . . has four very strong bastions, built of stone as are the walls, all well furnished with cannon. . . . In the rainy season it often happens that the low ground behind is covered with water. . . . The town is open. The houses are somewhat low and confined.[73]

We may guess, that the emblem on Mendis' tomb depicts the Dutch Fort Geldria at Pulicat. In any case, it represents one of the few sketches of a European seventeenth-century coastal trading settlement in south India. The tomb of Abraham Mendis' brother, Louis (d. 1686), who was buried on the Portuguese Cemetery at Pulicat two years later, depicts the image of the fortress—not as a front-image, but in a bird's-eye view perspective. What inspired the Mendes family to adopt an image of a European fortress (possibly of Geldria itself) instead of a traditional family emblem is not known. As no written sources could be ascertained, we may only assume, that it was the protection of the private enterprise a European fortress offered to a Portuguese family which generated moral obligation and affection and stimulated the choice of this unique sketch.

Next to the coats-of-arms, the border decorations of the Dutch ledgers bear witness to an increasing professionalism of Netherlandish sculpturing in south India between the mid-seventeenth and mid-eighteenth century as well. Seventeenth-century ledgers from the Netherlands, with the exception of a very few, do not boast border decorations. Notably the leaf-scrolls, which characterize the Dutch ledgers in Coromandel, are not to be found on ledgers in the Netherlands; but almost identical patterns were well known in the Netherlands as decorative objects in other contexts, for example, on furniture.[74] These decorations were well known in Europe itself, but it is not as such clear if they were of European origin as well.[75] A look onto the scrollwork around some coats-of-arms might be elusive: While the symbol itself is usually decorated by an image of cloth in European iconography, the cloth is converted into a leaf ornament by the Indian sculptor. This might be seen as an indicator that Indian craftsmen reinterpreted European decorations in the colonial context. We may thus assume that the specific decorations on the Dutch ledgers are the outcome of an Indo–European hybridization (Plates 20–23).

The border decorations represent different styles and were subject to significant alterations. A stylistic sequence can best be gleaned from an investigation of the Buitenkerkhof and the Binnenkerkhof at Pulicat. The oldest border decorations are characterized by scale-patterns. They were in use from the mid-1640s to the 1670s. During the 1650s, scrollwork made up of leaves or (rather seldom) flowers, appeared and featured the ledgers until the 1690s. More sophisticated patterns were in use from the 1670s and persisted until the 1720s. They are characterized by (rather seldom) two or (more common) three parallel ribbons. Scrollwork usually constituted the broader middle ribbon, whereas the edges of the decorations were featured by lines of squares (until 1720) and flowers (from 1710). A final stage of development was reached by Rococo-features from the 1730s, characterized by the versatile cherubs—symbolizing immortality[76]—amidst the scrollwork or at the corners of the border decorations. Interestingly, this latter pattern was taken up by British sculptors and was still in use at the onset of the nineteenth century, as transpires from a ledger on the Binnenkerkhof at Pulicat produced by de Rozario from Madras after 1829. The cherubs on the border decorations sometimes also correspond to cherubs decorating vertical funerary monuments. This notably applies to the monument created for Anna Margaretha Möller (d. 1737) at Pulicat. Cherubs are to be found on her ledger as well as on the mausoleum erected above the former.

The carving of the more sophisticated high relief in contrast to low relief appears to be another innovation of Dutch sculpturing in Coromandel next to the border decorations. The oldest inscriptions engraved in high relief from the 1670s survive on the Binnenkerkhof at Pulicat. High relief almost entirely ousted the low relief from Netherlandish cemeteries between Nagapattinam and Masulipatnam during the 1690s.

Next to the Dutch ledgers, the remaining English stone slabs of the Guava Garden from the latter half of the seventeenth and the first half of the eighteenth century constitute an important source and bear witness to colonial material culture. Similar to the Dutch, also English sepulchral craftsmanship in India developed its own style. In contrast to the commonly crude workmanship of monuments in England itself, the English memorials of Madras are characterized by a sophisticated and highly developed artistic work from about the 1690s. This feature does not only apply to a standardized architecture, border decoration and coats-of-arms, but also to the use of typographic, centred letters in contrast to the old calligraphic letters still to be found in England during that period.[77] The ledgers can rather be compared with contemporary Netherlandish monuments from India than with the produce at home—even if the Dutch in Coromandel had developed this sophisticated art of sculpturing almost half a century earlier than the English.

Most English ledgers from the abandoned Guava Garden, now preserved in front of St. Mary's Church at Fort St. George, from the decades prior to 1690 do not bear any border decoration at all or have just a plain, linear border.[78] The English border decorations that feature most ledgers from the last decade of the seventeenth century are similar to the Dutch ornaments, but are, however, not identical. The four corners of the decorations are usually set-off by separate edges and thus constitute individual squares. Flowers are more apparent in contrast to the prevailing leaves on the Dutch scrollwork. It may be surmised that the English decorations were stimulated by the Dutch produce in India, but that they were nevertheless created in different workshops. Furthermore, the early English stone slabs at Calcutta (St. John's Church) seem to be strongly influenced by English Coromandel sculpturing, however, even in this case, both schools are not identical.

Late medieval and early modern funerary culture in Europe was characterized by an increasing significance of death-symbolism representing the vanity of the human flesh. Such symbols of 'memento mori' served as reminders of the transiency of life and the inevitability of death and were created to induce self-reflection.[79] Commencing with thirteenth- to fifteenth-century so-called transi-tombs, these notions finally lead to an extensive symbolism comprising skull, bones, hour-glass, scythes or sexton's-tools in sculpture or print.[80] Such mortuary symbols were likewise quite common on English graves in south India, as the evidence from the Guava Garden suggests. About a quarter of the surviving ledgers—mainly from the period between 1690 and 1735—bears such symbols. While these symbols similarly were used in England from the end of the seventeenth century, they never became as popular here as in north-eastern America or in Scotland—and in India.[81] It was obviously the periphery of the growing English/British empire in the distance to the prevailing Anglican tradition (which only paid little attention to such death-symbolism), where symbols of mortality could gain a significant role.

Such symbols of mortality likewise prove to be of much less significance for the Dutch in south India. Only in very few instances 'memento-mori' symbolism features Dutch ledgers from Sadras or Nagapattinam between the 1690s and the 1790s. In contrast to south India, the remaining Dutch headstones from Colombo in Ceylon very well display mortuary symbols, which again underlines the fact that Coromandel created its own tradition of funerary architecture.[82] When such symbols were used on Dutch graves in Coromandel at all they were sometimes counterpoised by more conciliatory symbols like cherubs or consoling words ('Godt is Myn Heyl') as in the case of the monument for Anna Macharius (d. 1693) at Sadras. Against this backdrop, the gate of the Dutch Binnenkerkhof at Pulicat with a scull centred above the entrance and skeletons on its sides constitutes an exemption and quite an extraordinary example. The Dutch and Latin inscription from 1656 renders a virtual Calvinist attitude towards life and death: 'Beati Qui in Domino Moriuntur Quiescunt A Labore Suo. Apocolijps: Cap: xiv V: xiii.'

While the stone slab proves to be the prevailing type of monument before Neo-classical times according to the material evidence, vertical monuments can likewise be traced back to this period, however, only to a limited extent. When a burial ground was levelled down, only the ledgers appear to have survived, as in the case of the Guava Garden of Fort St. George or probably also of the Binnenkerkhof of Sadras. Considering the written evidence, this picture proves to be rather biased. When the English traveller Lockyer visited Fort St. George in 1711, he found representative vertical monuments inside the Guava Garden. He was in particular impressed by a number of 'lofty spires carved with different fancies after the Indian manner.[83] An investigation of the cemeteries from Surat, Bharuch or Ahmedabad in the northwest or the few remains at Balasore in Orissa contributes to this somewhat different picture of seventeenth-century vertical funerary architecture.[84]

It was notably the pyramid, the obelisk and the mausoleum, which featured the European cemeteries in south India next to the ledgers latest from the onset of the eighteenth century. The pyramid is of Egyptian origin and always functioned as a funerary monument. While the creation of wall-pyramids derives already from the Renaissance period, the free standing pyramid outside buildings seems to be a late seventeenth- and eighteenth-century European reception of the Roman Cestius-pyramid and its Egyptian predecessors. However, it was only from Piranesi's and Fischer von Erlach's times, that the pyramid increasingly gained more importance for architecture, even if the pyramid is already quite often depicted on seventeenth-century paintings.

Pyramids have been created on European cemeteries in India likewise from the end of the seventeenth century. Early examples are the remains of two pyramids on the Dutch burial ground at Balasore (Orissa), one of them commemorating Michellians Burggraaf van Sevenhuisen, who died in November 1696. The oldest remaining pyramids in the south are much younger, but they nevertheless precede the period of Neo-classicism. They first appear as decoration elements on the mausoleum of Anna Margaretha Möller (d. 1737), where four of them are placed on the top of the corners of the edifice close to the base of the cupola. Similar decorations are to be found on the seventeenth-century Dutch and English mausoleums from Surat, which might have constituted a model for south India. An individual pyramid in the south is only preserved from the second half of the eighteenth century by the monument of Sara Antonia de Goede (d. 1793) at Pulicat.

In contrast to the pyramid, the obelisk tapers towards the top. It is similarly not of Roman, but of ancient Egyptian origin. During the Roman and the medieval periods, the pyramid was regarded as a symbol of power and victory, and was rarely related to death. Only from the end of the fifteenth century, the sources mention obelisks as grave monuments in Europe itself. Monuments themselves are, however, only preserved from the latter half of the sixteenth century, such as the memorial for the Earl of Southampton in Titchfield/Hampshire (1592) or for William the Silent in Delft (begun 1614).[85] Obelisks were similarly a common feature in Netherlandish art during the latter half of the seventeenth century. They are not only to be found as decorative elements on paintings, but likewise appear as fayence table decorations.[86] They feature many eighteenth-century European memorials inside churches as well, but are to be found in larger numbers on the cemeteries in Europe only from the end of that century—later gaining a plain and simple shape under the impact of the architecture of the French Revolution.[87]

On the Dutch and English burial grounds of northwest India, obelisks are to be found already during the seventeenth century, which appears to be very early in the European context. One early obelisk, most likely from the 1720s, survives on 'Karikop' at Nagapattinam bearing the inscription plates of Adriana Catharina Pla (d. 1721) and Adriana Appels (d. 1743) and three of her children. This obelisk does not resemble the seventeenth- and early eighteenth-century obelisks from the Dutch cemeteries of Surat or Bharuch with their large pediments and a more 'oriental' appearance. It instead resembles the more classical European type, which is still to be found on the European cemeteries of Bengal belonging to the latter half of the eighteenth century.

Next to pyramids and obelisks, the mausoleum likewise constituted an eminent type of funerary monument in Indian cemeteries from the latter half of the seventeenth century. Named after the funerary monument Queen Artemisia erected for her husband, Mausolos, in the fourth century BC, the mausoleum is an independent, roofed funerary monument. It regained importance during the Italian Renaissance finally to feature eighteenth- and nineteenth-century European burial and landscape architecture.[88] It has been argued by Curl, that it was not just European taste, but north Indian Muslim architecture as well, which influenced the creation of European mausoleums in India and in Great Britain. Drawing upon the magnificent Mughal funerary architecture, European merchants in Surat and Bharuch were the first to be commemorated by huge mausoleums displaying a hybrid European Mughal style from the latter half of the seventeenth century. The need for representation within the most eminent seaports of the Mughal empire obviously necessitated such an opulent style, while the monuments from Surat commemorating the Oxenden brothers (d. 1659 and 1669) and of Hendrik Adriaan, Baron van Reede (d. 1691) usually serve as the most prominent examples. These edifices obviously later constituted the models for a number of monuments for British families from Northern Ireland having close ties with India, such as transpires from the late eighteenth-century Indian-style mausoleums at Knockbreda.[89] And they likewise influenced John Vanbrugh's treatises on cemetery architecture and gardening, who had sojourned in Surat during the 1680s.[90]

Even if no seventeenth-century mausoleum survives in the European cemeteries in south India, several indicators point towards their former existence. At first we discover a striking similarity between Lockyer's expression of 'lofty spires' to be found inside the Guava Garden near Fort St. George and John Vanbrugh's claim for 'Lofty and Noble Mausoleums' for a future British funerary architecture—an idea he obviously had picked up from the European monuments at Surat.[99] Another source likewise unveils this assumption: A rough sketch of the Nyegade Kirkegaard at Danish Tranquebar is preserved on the Tranquebar map of Gregers Daa Trellund from 1733, which actually displays Tranquebar of the 1690s. Apart from a number of tomb-like monuments, it shows a vertical structure made of columns and arches and topped by a small cupola resembling a mausoleum.[92]

A limited number of mausoleums indeed survives along the Coromandel Coast from the first half of the eighteenth century. The oldest existing monument belongs to Anthonia Nilo, wife of the Dutch governor of Coromandel. She died in 1709 and was buried alongside four of her children on the Karikop at Nagapattinam. A ledger is situated inside a huge mausoleum with a cupola, which is decorated by bowls. On top of the four arches emblems showing Fortuna, which are supported by two cherubs each, are to be found. Among the oldest surviving mausoleums is also the grave of Jan Martensz, the chief of the Dutch factory at Pulicat, who died in 1717 and was buried in the Binnenkerkhof. This monument displays a very coarse structure with one arch at the front, one at the back and two arches on the sides. The entire structure is comparatively low. It is topped by a barrel roof and seven pediments, probably the basements for urns or pots. Similarly stocky architecture is neither to be found at Surat nor Bharuch. It has more likely been influenced by south Indian Indo–European military and civil architecture which transpires from the remains of the fortified factories in Coromandel such as Dansborg at Tranquebar.

The already mentioned monument commemorating Anna Margaretha Möller (d. 1737) renders another example (Plate 24). The mausoleum with its square ground-plan exhibits three arches on each side. The corner-pillars are topped by pyramids, while additional top parts are to be found around the basement of the cupola and above it. The pediments are decorated on three sides with crowned coats of arms, cherubs and scrollwork. A ledger is placed on the ground inside the monument. Even if smaller in size, the structure and decoration with pyramids and urn- or pot-like items clearly correspond to the shape of the Dutch and English monuments in the seventeenth-century cemeteries of Surat and Bharuch in their distinct Mughal–European hybrid style. The similarities support the impression of the transfer of architectural designs—if not of the architects themselves—between the European settlements in northwest India and Coromandel.

The Neo-classical Period

The last decades of the eighteenth and the first half of the nineteenth century brought about a variety of architectural styles in the cemeteries in Europe and abroad, and according to Colvin, representing a virtual 'stylistic anarchy'.[93] It proves a futile task to categorize all the various monuments, which spread in larger numbers than ever before across the European cemeteries in south India during this time. Nevertheless, a rough sketch may be outlined here.

The decades after about 1770 are not simply characterized by Neo-classicism with its distinct moulding of Romanesque architecture. Monuments created in the Egyptian manner, such as obelisks and pyramids, still retained a prominent position, whereas the early edifices, created according to Neo-Gothic style, simultaneously appear in the cemeteries. Early modern structures, such as the ledgers, witnessed a revival in the south. A common feature of the entire period is the gradual disappearance of the Indo–European hybrid architecture, which characterized a number of monuments during earlier periods. Now, European cemeteries in India became even more 'European'.

The European Neo-classical funerary architecture drew its inspiration from the rediscovery of the ancient world as well as from the current enlightened discourses. From the late 1720s, and inspired by Pietro Santi Santoli's work *Antichi Sepolchri* (1697), classical Greek, Roman or Egyptian monuments such as mausolea, tomb-chests, sarcophagi, cippi, pillars, pedestal tombs, obelisks and pyramids featured in garden architecture in England as decorative elements. These were later also to be found on the continent inside the *jardin Anglais*.[94] The subsequent rediscovery of ancient sculptures and early archaeological excavations at Pompeii and Herculaneum during the latter half of the eighteenth century furthered such reshaping of European taste and architecture and paved the way for the enduring success of Neo-classicism. Ancient funeral monuments in particular raised the interest of intellectuals and poets and brought about an enormous number of publications. The design of such monuments was not only described and interpreted, but it was likewise debated how authentically to put them into practice again. Against this backdrop, Johann Joachim Winckelmann's *Gedanken über die Nachahmung der griechischen Werke in der Malerey und Bildhauerkunst* (1755, English edn. in 1765) paved the way for a broad discourse on ancient arts and influenced a whole generation.[95] The same applies to the work of Gotthold Ephraim Lessing, who exhaustively—but not uncontested—investigated the symbolism of ancient funerary sculpture in his famous book *Wie die Alten den Tod gebildet* (1769). In England, it was especially the works of Chambers, as well as of Robert and James

Adam, which propagated the new architectural taste,[96] and in France it was the sketches of architects like Jardin, Le Geay and Boullée.[97] Roman and Greek architecture and symbolism were soon adopted by artisans and painters, most impressively by Canova, Thorvaldsen and Wiedewelt, the creators of famous tomb monuments.[98]

In south India, this new style turned up in three different phases. A first period of Neo-classical architecture, from the 1770s to about 1800, transpires from the edifices of St. Mary's Cemetery at Madras, from the cemeteries at Tranquebar and from the Dutch Cemetery at Cochin.[99] However, since Madras had been eclipsed by the tremendous wealth of Bengal, resulting from trade and tax-income during the latter half of the eighteenth century, it was mainly Calcutta which brought about the larger and more sophisticated monuments during this time.[100] While the South Park Street Cemetery at Calcutta soon must have resembled a virtual necropolis, the monuments from Madras, Tranquebar and Cochin generally were smaller and lower. It was mainly the tomb-chests of about 1 m height, which dominated Neo-classical funerary architecture in the south before 1800. A common feature was their decoration with simple or more elaborate Neo-classical pilaster strips. Tomb-chests often served as substructures for a stone slab, whilst in other instances, the inscription-plate was affixed to the side of the monuments.[101] Closely related to the tomb-chest is the simple Neo-classical sarcophagus with pilaster strips and with a curved lid, which likewise characterizes the decades after 1770. However, this type can by no means be compared with the elaborate Romanesque sarcophagi from mid-nineteenth century. All these monuments were made of brick and plaster—most probably painted white—to imitate marble.[102]

Next to these ubiquitous edifices, which were widespread across south India, two distinct types of architecture obviously emerged only at Cochin during the last decades of the eighteenth century. One type was featured by Rococo ornaments like scrollwork and shells such as on an ostentatious sarcophagus from 1784. In a few instances it is found that the British adopted such shell decoration at Cochin even during the first half of the nineteenth century.

Another very distinct and enduring type of a tomb-monument was also developed in Dutch Cochin during this period. It is characterized by a sub-construction with pilaster strips and a linear or curved lid, in itself resembling a tomb-chest or sarcophagus. On top of it, a geometrical coffin made of brickwork is placed. This model was retained during the early British period of Cochin after 1825 and was further developed in other places.[103] While the coffin on the top of the monument as well as the pilaster strips at the corners and the sides disappeared soon after, the curved sub-structure survived independently as a sarcophagus during the 1830s. This model also spread to the Coromandel Coast, where it is still to be found in the European cemetery at Porto Novo.

This quite plain and humble early Neo-classical architecture was replaced by a new trend favouring higher vertical monuments like pillars, temples or pedestal monuments between about 1800 and 1830. While such fashion had already been well established in the European cemeteries of Bengal from the latter half of the eighteenth century, it reached the south in only about 1800. And it was not the British but obviously the French at Pondicherry who served as the trendsetter. We may well presume that the French in India drew on the architectural expertise of their mother country. It was the cemetery of Père-Lachaise at Paris indeed, which attracted a large number of foreign tourists from the onset of the nineteenth century and which stimulated publications on Neo-classical funerary architecture and pattern books. Even if only less than half of the monuments created in Père-Lachaise between 1804 and 1816 were of larger dimensions and resembling Neo-classical structures (columns, pillars or sarcophagi)'[104] they doubtlessly shaped the character of this burial ground. This cemetery also created the model for other modern cemeteries like Mount Jerome at Dublin, Kensal Green at London or the Glasgow Necropolis[105]—and also to the French cemeteries in India. An early example of the transfer of Neo-classical monumental patterns from the mother country to India during the second period is provided by the tomb-monument commemorating Michel Joachim Raymond, the French mercenary commander of the Nizam of Hyderabad. He died in 1798 for reasons as yet unexplained. After his death, a monument was created on a hilltop near Hyderabad, close to the French cantonment, comprising a Greek temple and a large pyramid likewise displaying the influence of French revolutionary architecture.[106]

On the burial ground of Pondicherry at Cholas Nagar, south of the town centre, early tomb-chests and smaller pedestal tombs survive from the 1780s. This still quite humble Neo-classical architecture received a tremendous impetus right from the onset of the nineteenth century (Plate 25). Still, during the period of the British occupation at the time of the Napoleonic Wars, new vertical Neo-classical monuments of much larger dimensions spread across the cemetery. Even if these monuments were smaller in size and less elaborate than in Paris, the entire ensemble soon must have produced a similar image of a necropolis with geometrical features and shady alleys. This new style was not only based upon the architecture of the monuments but upon the latest decorative style on the inscription-plates. It is notable that the elaborate and vertical Neo-classical architecture at Cholas Nagar precedes the Neo classical architectural construction of houses at Pondicherry itself from 1816 for about a decade.[107] However, despite its modern appearance, mortuary symbols such as bones and skulls are still to be found in Pondicherry (as well as in other places)[108] during this time, rendering the artistic transfer from Baroque symbolism to Neo-classicism a long and inconsistent process.

In contrast to Pondicherry, Dutch Cochin and British Madras remained quite conservative during the first decades of the nineteenth century. They still witnessed the old features characterized by ledgers and tomb-chests (some of them were now decorated with urns; however, most of the urns have perished in the course of time). The only vertical monuments of larger dimension were the obelisks and pyramids on Neo-classical pedestal structures, which drew on late seventeenth- and eighteenth-century Egyptian style. These burial grounds must rather have left the impression more of an open and spacious ground than of a necropolis. The same picture is presented by the English cemetery at Madurai. With the single exception of a vertical monument, only ledgers and very simple pedestal constructions survive from the first two decades of the nineteenth century.

Apart from obelisks and pyramids, already well known during the entire eighteenth century, vertical Neo-classical constructions are extremely rare in St. Mary's Cemetery at Madras. An example from among only three remaining mausolea is represented by the cenotaph for the Hope family, whose members all drowned in 1809. Instead of the hybrid style of the eighteenth-century mausoleums from Pulicat, the monument now has an entirely Neo-classical appearance with four sarcophagi decorating the corners of the cornice replacing the Baroque pyramids to be found at Pulicat. Similar sarcophagi crowning an arched substructure (however, in another architectural context) are to be found on the Darnley mausoleum designed by James Wyatt in *c.* 1783–4.[109]

Compared with Madras, the burial grounds at Tranquebar of the Neo-classical period proved to be quite exceptional. Due to a comparatively small number of European inhabitants, the Danes at Tranquebar never felt compelled to establish a cemetery outside the town walls. The development of its burial grounds into modern nineteenth-century cemeteries therefore took place inside the town. Similar to Madras, the new Neo-classical trend had only gradually reached Tranquebar. Compared with the other European trading settlements in Coromandel, most vertical monuments in the cemeteries of Tranquebar are quite small. This feature might be due to the fact that space was obviously limited inside the town walls, since the grounds could not be extended at will. Furthermore, the quite modest appearance of the monuments coincides with an economic decline of the Danish settlement at Tranquebar from the end of the eighteenth century.[110] At Tranquebar, the final decades of the eighteenth century are still characterized by ledgers, most of them placed on tomb-chests. During the first three decades of the nineteenth century, different kinds of development took place depending on the social composition of the individual cemetery in Tranquebar. It was notably the more prestigious churchyard of the Zion Church which witnessed the early creation of vertical Neo-classical monuments. Here, pedestal monuments with obelisks or pillars were created before 1820.[111] The Nyegade Kirkegaard, with a notably larger number of interments of the middle and lower classes, witnessed this development only from the 1830s with a focus on pedestal monuments with urns and also pillars.[112] The churchyard of the New Jerusalem Church—the church of the German missionaries from Halle—shows an even more modest appeal. Apart from three vertical Neo-classical designs,[113] most monuments were ledgers situated on the ground or on low tomb-chests or were simple sarcophagi. Even if the total number of Neo-classical monuments on the cemeteries of Tranquebar is quite small, our observation might indicate, that it was not only the geographical situation but also the social spectrum of the interred in the individual cemeteries, which influenced the introduction of Neo-classical funerary architecture in south India.

Next to the quite standardized monuments, the Nyegade Kirkegaard at Tranquebar exhibits two exceptional monuments, which unfortunately cannot be dated. Both of them feature pediments, one with a coffin made of brick, the other with a vault behind. The first pediment represents a columned doorway with three arches in relief. The four indicated pillars are each topped by a pyramidal element. Above them, a cornice supports the triangular top of the pediment. It is decorated by two dragons resembling an s-curve.[114] The pediment of the latter monument only boasts one arch and is again topped by s-shaped decorations (Plate 26).[115] These decorations still seem to represent a hybrid form of architecture composed of European features (like Doric pillars, arches and pyramids) and a kind of supposedly 'Oriental' style characterized by dragons and s-curves. The hybrid style might have been influenced by the architecture of the nearby New Jerusalem Church with similar roof-decorations. The pediments themselves emulate a mausoleum with pillars, arches and the characteristic pyramids. Due to a lack of funds or space such edifices might have been constructed here instead of the erection of virtual mausoleums.

From the 1830s, i.e. during the third phase, the Neo-classical style was further developed, particularly in the British settlements. While the French cemeteries, especially Père-Lachaise, had constituted a model for Pondicherry immediately after 1800, it was the British garden-cemetery promoted by Loudon, which stimulated the shaping of new cemeteries and funerary architecture in Great Britain and India from the second third of the nineteenth century.

St. Stephen's Church Cemetery at Ootacamund in particular provides a good example. It is not only the geometrical layout of the ground, dividing it into several plots, but also the construction of solid podiums for larger pedestal tombs and sarcophagi, which, according to Loudon, prevented their sagging into the ground (as many monuments did, for example, at Highgate in London), which characterizes the funerary architecture at Ootacamund from the 1840s.[116] Furthermore, Loudon insisted on the protection of cemeteries by high walls to prevent vandalism which gave rise to the creation of walls around most British burial grounds in India and iron fences around individual monuments from the 1830s.

The architecture itself also witnessed a refinement from the 1830s, which was, however, confined to a small number of outstanding examples. Virtual Romanesque models are rarely found from the 1830s, and they are generally restricted to the social and commercial elites. St. Stephen's Churchyard at Ootacamund exhibits a few examples. A sarcophagus with Roman pedestals, for example, commemorates Albert and Catherine Frend.[117] Albert Frend was doubtlessly one of the most reputed and commercially active members of the local European society. Not only did he introduce new varieties of fruits at his orchard in Snowdon near Ootacamund, but he also founded the Llangollen Brewery near Marlimand.[118]

Slightly more popular on the south Indian cemeteries than the Romanesque sarcophagi was the Romanesque altar-tomb, which spread across large portions of Europe and the New World between the 1830s and 1860s.[119] Due to its smaller dimensions compared with the Romanesque sarcophagus, it was generally made of natural stone such as marble or granite. Two identical altar-tombs decorated with cloths falling in folds, commemorating Hannah Maria Mason (d. 1838) and Samuel Mason (d. 1867), in St. Mary's Cemetery in Madras, serve as good examples. The marble altar-tomb commemorating William Graham McIvor in St. Stephen's Cemetery similarly represents a landmark. It imitates the Roman tomb of Cornelius Scipio Barbatus and is characterized by a cartouche with the inscription and a front-relief showing four twigs with leaves and flowers. Next to the flowers acting as a symbol of remembrance, they might recall McIvor's career as a Kew-trained horticulturalist, who was Manager of the Government Garden at Ootacamund from 1848.[120]

Just as the Romanesque sarcophagi, the cippi, originating from border stones of Roman burial grounds or depositories for ashes, are unusually to be found on European cemeteries in south India.[121] Two rare examples are, for instance, in the Zion Church Cemetery of Danish Tranquebar from mid-nineteenth century.[122]

Quite an extraordinary type of funerary monument of the Neo-classical period survives in the European cemetery of Madurai from the first half of the nineteenth century resembling the so-called bale-tombs. This type originates from late seventeenth-century England, but is quite rare in colonial India. It is mainly restricted to Balasore (Orissa) and more impressively to Madurai, where a number of them survives from the nineteenth century. Round, black, polished stones are inserted horizontally and also vertically into brick-monuments. In one case, a monument—which is simultaneously the oldest of this type dating back to 1804—resembles a kind of canopy yielding an image of a well or a stove with a chimney. While only very few monuments of this type survive from the first two decades of the nineteenth century, they seem to have been particularly popular between the 1820s and the beginning of the 1840s. However, one monument was erected as late as 1864. It seems not to have been very likely that the British at Madurai developed an individual architectural style for aesthetic reasons. An investigation of the other, contemporary monuments, such as the ledgers, leaves the impression that the types of locally available stone used for ledgers were of a coarse structure and not very suitable for inscriptions. They usually only enabled the engraving of very rough inscriptions and not elaborate decorations. The nicely polished round inscription-stones of the bale-tombs stand in sharp contrast to these monuments of the same period. It may be suggested here that the English—for want of suitable natural stones for inscription-plates—took away the pillars from Indian edifices to create these monuments.

Whereas almost all inscription-plates in south India of this period were made of some kind of natural stone, a number of cast iron plates survives on brick monuments in the European cemetery at Porto Novo (Parangipettai). They had been cast during the 1830s in memory of the wife of a civil engineer, a smelter, a plate-roller, a puddler and a skingler—formerly employees of an ill-fated British iron-works enterprise there.[123] A tradition is maintained here, which finds its origin in sixteenth-century England, where cast iron inscription-plates were created in regions with substantial iron production such as Herefordshire or Shropshire.[124]

THE PERIOD OF GOTHIC REVIVAL AND MODERN STYLES

From the 1840s, the architecture of the monuments became even more diverse in England, on the continent and abroad—a trend dominating the south Indian cemeteries from about the 1860s. Next to the traditional ledgers and still surviving Neo-classical models, Gothic-medieval, Egyptian as well as modernist, geometrical structures appear during the latter half of the nineteenth century. This variety of styles was only replaced in the 1890s by a domination of plain crosses and headstones—often surrounded by kerbs—as the prevailing style of the first half of the twentieth century. Nevertheless, two major trends, which provide this period with a unique character may be discovered: The Gothic revival and the Egyptian revival.

In contrast to the preceding Neo-classical style, Neo-Gothic architecture favoured headstones, crosses, or low profile sarcophagi. It is furthermore characterized by a distinct decoration of the monuments imitating Gothic-medieval architecture. Common features are crockets, trefoils, quatrefoils, foliated crosses and tracery. Multicolour effects on the monuments or inscription-plates were also popular.[125] A large number of monuments, especially crosses or headstones, features the letters IHS—the first three letters of the Greek lettering of Jesus. During the second half of the nineteenth century, flowers as decorative objects also became popular as symbols of remembrance.[126] Gothic revival is not only evident from the monuments themselves, but also from the architecture of the cemetery buildings, especially the entrance gates and chapels. In the south Indian cemeteries, purely Gothic monuments are comparatively rare. The Gothic style is mainly confined to headstones emulating Gothic pediments[127] or to Gothic letters—such as on low profile sarcophagi—and decoration. These are usually fewer in number by the continuing construction of Neo-classical edifices and even more by plain, modernist structures such as plain crosses or headstones. In south India, Neo-Gothic buildings or cemetery gates are still found at the entrances to St. Mary's as well as Kilpauk Cemetery in Madras and St. Stephen's churchyard of Ootacamund (Plate 27). The former, in particular, respects Loudon's appeal for entrance-lodges 'to comprise a room to serve as an office to contain the cemetery book, or at least, the order book and register . . .'.[128]

The Egyptian style was not entirely new during the nineteenth century. As mentioned earlier in this chapter, pyramids and obelisks were common in European as well as in Indian cemeteries from the latter half of the seventeenth century. During the nineteenth century, they became more popular not just in their earlier monumental size and design, but also as smaller structures sometimes less than 1 m high. In the European cemeteries in India, they still constitute—howsoever small—a proportion of the total number of monuments, but their distinct features lead to their becoming landmarks within the burial grounds.

The latter half of the nineteenth century not only brought about a fundamental change of architecture but, at the same time, of the choice of material. During the first decades of the nineteenth century, most of the vertical monuments were made of brick, while from the 1840s, polished natural stones became common. While bricks were always readily available, natural stones in many instances had to be transported over long distances (sometimes as far as from Europe) and were accordingly more expensive—a visible outcome of an increased price was the fact that the monuments became smaller.

The nineteenth century thus witnessed the broadest variety of architectural styles in the European cemeteries in south India. An attempt at statistical differentiation may be made by using the evidence from St. Stephen's Churchyard at Ootacamund.

Figure 27 classifies the surviving monuments in three groups: 1. Ledgers deriving their origin from Early Modern times. 2. Neo-classical monuments, such as tomb-chests, pedestals and sarcophagi. 3. Crosses and headstones of a Neo-Gothic and geometrical style as well as Egyptian revival monuments.

The figure clearly indicates the fact, that the Neo-classical monuments by far outnumbered the other types until the 1860s. They dominated St. Stephen's Church Cemetery especially during the 1840s. During this period, sarcophagi were most prominent (19) followed by tomb-chests (12) and pedestals (11). Other Neo-classical monuments were of lesser significance such as pedimental designs (3), pyramids (2) and obelisks in a Neo-classical manner (1). Each type of these monuments varies in size and quality from a very simple masonry to early, but elaborate marble edifices. While Neo-classical monuments still dominated the 1850s, two other trends become visible: a renaissance of the traditional ledgers which persisted still during the 1960s, and the appearance of crosses and headstones, which prevailed during the final decades of the nineteenth and the first half of the twentieth century in the European cemeteries in India. The ledgers now appear in a refined shape

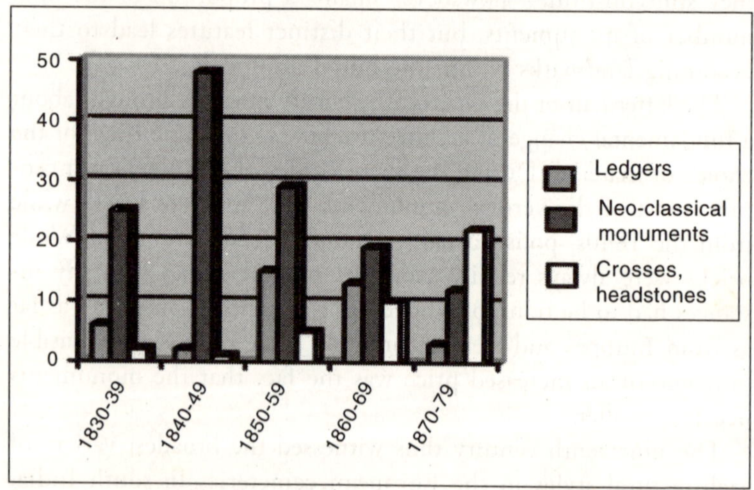

Figure 27: Types of monuments on St. Stephen's Church Cemetery, Ootacamund (1830–79)

and mostly polished, and they are still today created for the cemeteries at Ootacamund and other places in smaller numbers. Neo-classical monuments gradually lost importance finally to be replaced by crosses and headstones during the 1870s.

The European Cemetery at Kotagiri, with interments from the 1820s till today, proves a useful complement to St. Stephen's Church Cemetery at Ootacamund. The few remaining monuments of the first half of the nineteenth century are exclusively dominated by Neo-classical architecture. The latter half of that century displays a mixture of ledgers, crosses with and without kerbs and already one headstone from the 1890s. The dominant form of the first half of the twentieth century is the cross on a podium made of two or three steps inside a kerb. Headstones surrounded by kerbs are also common and gained the largest acceptance during the 1950s, while other types, like sarcophagi and scrolls without kerbs, are less common. A striking feature of the mid-twentieth century is a second Renaissance of the ledger at Kotagiri. Ledgers do not appear until the 1850s, and only a small number is to be found at Kotagiri between the 1860s and 1880. No ledger exists from 1890 to 1919, whereas they gain great popularity from the 1920s again to emerge as the most accepted type of monument after Independence, during the 1950s and 1960s. The ledger thus emerges as the most enduring funerary monument of colonial south India covering half a millennium of funerary architecture on the subcontinent, but it was, however, always subject to distinct fashions and taste.

INSCRIPTIONS

Inscriptions constitute relevant elements of memorial culture as well.[129] They are an image of people's self-perception and transcend the biological limits of life. Inscriptions were usually engraved in stone—the most enduring material—and rarely in timber or cast in iron as, for example, in Porto Novo. An investigation of the inscriptions which survive on the European cemeteries in south India, clearly reveal different periods of style, contents and philosophy.

The necessity to pray for the deceased and to recommend their souls to God was a firm topos from the Medieval period. Already during the ninth century, Pope Nicolaus II had stipulated the need to erect a visible grave-monument to keep the memory of a deceased person alive.[130] However, personal data were initially of little importance in Europe, and the year or date of demise is mentioned in inscriptions only from the fifteenth century onwards. In sixteenth- and seventeenth-century Catholic Europe the inscriptions could finally turn out to be a virtual narrative of someone's life—a development, which was obviously not shared by the Portuguese monuments in India, but more by the Dutch monuments.

The sincere wish to immortalize oneself or someone's relatives by inscription initially opposed the Christian ideal of vanity of any earthly asset; but individual desire regularly proved to be more dominating than theological demand, which is already noticed by Sir Thomas Browne's 'Urne Buriall' in 1658.[131] To justify personalized inscriptions, they thus had to serve a proper purpose. As early as 1618, Richard Brathwayte mentions two types of inscriptions which may be perceived as justifiable even in a theological sense: the moral ('such as to induce instruction') and the religious ('grave and divinely moving sentences').[132]

Reality on the monuments itself, however, proved to be somewhat different—in Europe as well as in colonial India. In many instances, inscriptions just tend to reflect the worldly essence of someone's life, which transpires—for instance—from the inscription on William and Ann Higgins' monument who both died in 1877 in Ootacamund in the Nilgiris:

> They were two of the first settlers on these hills,
> who from humble circumstances
> raised themselves to a position
> that won the respect and esteem of all.

In this case, worldly succees emerges as the essence of life.

The creation of monuments and inscriptions was subject to the secular changes of taste and varying notions of death. They thus not only constitute a testimony for an individual person but even more (albeit unwillingly) for their time, space and culture. They simultaneously unveil prevailing virtues, religiosity and notions of the meaning of life and offer unique insights into differing attitudes towards death.[133] Most inscriptions from the European cemeteries in south India are thus standardized in accordance to their time of creation and do not seem to be as individualistic as suggested by Guthke.[134] Moreover, the inscriptions not only mirror contemporary virtues and individual self-perception, but simultaneously record the names, age and year of death, family, profession and social position, which also render them an eminent demographic source.

Generally, we can distinguish two types of inscriptions: *prospective* and *retrospective* ones. The inscriptions from the European cemeteries in south India share the European trend of prospective inscriptions until the last decades of the eighteenth century. These inscriptions generally focus on the after-life of the deceased, while worldly merits are not mentioned at all or (as in the case of the Calvinists) are recorded to underline the prospects for a blessed afterlife. They generally feature the desire for prayers ('Orate pro eo'—pray for him) or for a later resurrection.

From the sixteenth century onwards, the Portuguese in India usually preferred a very plain language, and the surviving inscriptions only yield meagre information on the person interred. Portuguese inscriptions survive, for example, at Cochin, Goa as well as in today's Madras (San Tomé Cathedral and Luz Church). In many instances, we only come to know the name of the deceased and of his wife or children. Not every ledger mentions the year of death, and in only very few instances the age of demise or profession. Most inscriptions follow a standardized pattern; the text usually starts with the phrase 'Sepultura De' (monument of), which is followed by the name of the deceased, the name of his wife and children and (rarely) the date as well as (more common) the year of death. Instead of the real name of his wife and children, the inscriptions in many instances only unveil the standardizes phrase 'and to his/their heirs', who might have been buried here as well: '. . . e de seus herdeiros.' Such words can be regarded as an indicator, that the tomb was conceived as a family-grave right from the outset. However, if the heirs really were buried here cannot be contended any more. We may well presume, that these scanty inscriptions reflect the Roman Catholic attitude towards death, which departs from a mere transcendental, prospective basis. This impression is supported by our observations from the Catholic cemetery at Cholas Nagar, formerly French Pondicherry. Here, even most inscriptions from the nineteenth century still feature the headlines 'Ici repose', 'Ci Git' or are even without any headline at all.

Seventeenth- and eighteenth-century Dutch inscriptions usually prove to be much more elusive. Next to the name of the deceased, his profession is mentioned, very often the exact date of birth, the date as well as the age of death—mostly mentioned by years, sometimes also by the month and day. Also, the place of birth is recorded quite often, and in a few instances the cause of death. We may therefore conclude, that the Dutch, like the English and the Danish inscriptions, generally render much more information for the historian and the genealogist than the Portuguese. It is to be presumed, that the abundance of information especially on the Dutch ledgers coincides with the contemporary Calvinist idea of predestination: Success in someone's profession and accumulation of wealth were perceived as an indicator of being destined to heaven in the afterlife. An entirely different attitude towards one's own life transpires from this religious perception in contrast to the Roman Catholic one.

Nevertheless, the Dutch inscriptions of the seventeenth and eighteenth centuries also reflect the old, prospective type of inscription. Most inscriptions start with the standardized phrase 'Hier leijt begraven . . ' (At this place is buried). Instead of 'begraven', we also find the term 'Her under rust . . ', which means, someone 'rests' here—we may add: until his or her resurrection. The early English inscriptions unveil a similar attitude towards life and death. Almost all inscriptions from the old Guava Garden at Fort St. George start with the headlines 'Here Lyeth Interred the Body of'. The verb 'lyeth' indicates the temporariness of physical death and the perspective of getting unified with the eternal soul at a later time.

Nevertheless, the inscriptions from the Guava Garden simultaneously reveal a gradual change from a prospective to a retrospective view towards death as early as from late seventeenth century. They bear witness to a shift towards highlighting worldly virtues and success as an example for the surviving. Most inscriptions of the Guava Garden from that period still bear the phrase 'Here Lyeth Interred the Body of . . .', followed by the name of the deceased and the date of death, sometimes also mentioning the age of the deceased and the names of close relatives. However, these phrases were successively complemented by worldly issues such as highlighting moral virtues or career. The most impressive example of such a change of perspective may be found on the ledger commemorating Nathaniel Foxcroft at the Guava Garden:

Here lyeth the body of
Nathaniel Foxcroft/
Son of/
George Foxcroft Agent and /
Governor in Fort S George /
He was borne in to this world the 6 of September 1635 and /
Translated into a better to
The resurrection of the just the 26 of October 1670
After he had finished his pilgrimage on the earth 35
Yeares having allwaies
Exhibited all the honour due
From a dear son to his parents and by his universal obliging &
Ingeneous conversation
Obtained a good report &
Left a good name with
All men.

This inscription already displays the allegedly brilliant social reputation Foxcroft had enjoyed among his family and others, but still refers to the older idea of the transitory nature of life symbolized by the term 'pilgrimage' here. Even shorter, but in a similar sense, reads another inscription:

Here lyes interrd ye body
Of Capt Anthony Williams
A Britton
A person respected in his
Life for his true courage

Honour & integrity. He
Dyed the 8th of Novemb.
1691.

Anne Fowke, who died in Madras in 1734, is described as 'irreproachable, blameless, and unspotted'.

From the onset of the eighteenth century, the social position and careers are mentioned in an increasing number on English and Dutch inscriptions. Individual features and personal feelings of grief become visible despite a reference to the old, optimistic perspective regarding a later resurrection.

The transfer from the prospective to the retrospective type of inscription proved to be tremendously long-winded. The image of the dead body sleeping, resting or lying until its resurrection and reunification with the eternal soul proved to be extremely persistent despite new ideas of Enlightenment and worldly virtues, which gained prominence during the eighteenth century. Only from the end of the eighteenth century, a more modern notion of memory and commemoration increasingly replaced the Early Modern headlines in the inscriptions. An investigation of the English inscriptions from St. Mary's Cemetery of Madras shows that during the 1780s, most inscriptions still start with the phrases 'Here Lyeth Interred . . .' or 'Here Lyeth the Body of . . .'. The last inscription of the old type commemorates an infant daughter of Captain and Mrs. Straham, who died in 1827.

However, the last two decades of the eighteenth century simultaneously witnessed a striking change in the character of the inscriptions of many monuments. While the traditional phrase 'Here Lieth the Body of . . .' lost importance, it was gradually replaced by the new 'In Memory of . . .', which expresses a rather retrospective perception focusing on the individual or collective memory of the deceased.

The retrospective inscription corresponds to the emerging Neoclassic architecture, which embarks on ancient Roman ideas and highlights the life, virtues or the career of the deceased.[135] These new worldly inscriptions displayed virtues and beauty, until they were fully themselves replaced by Romantic or (later) Victorian notions of grief. A characteristic inscription commemorates 21-years old Matilda Hardyman, who had died in 1804, eulogizing her appearance and her character:

. . . who
with the softer beauties of the Sex
Kindness of Heart and Openness of Manner
possessed a Mind
enlightened and correct
a quick Perception
and an Utterance lively and natural
as the thought conceived . . .

'An enlightened Mind' symbolizes the major goal of an epoch, which just then was about to come to an end—the Age of Enlightenment.

The retrospective view from the decades around 1800 was later increasingly replaced by an individualistic terminology focusing on very personal feelings. The personal memory and grief of the surviving, which is recorded by mid-nineteenth-century inscriptions, sometimes displays a very family-centred attitude such as in the case of James Ferguson, who had died in 1836 and was buried on St. Mary's Cemetery at Madras. It is to be read, that

This Monument is erected
by his disconsolate Widow
to perpetuate the Memory
of one of the best Husbands
the kindest of Fathers
and the sincerest of Friends.

On top of the monument, the inscription 'Vault' is affixed. The monument was obviously dedicated as a family-vault, however, only one person was finally interred here. An increasing individualism nevertheless still proved to be a chiefly male issue. During the nineteenth century, married women were usually defined as wives and only to a much lesser degree as independent individuals. In many instances, name and occupation of the husband were mentioned on the inscriptions commemorating their wives. In a few instances, a widow was not more than her 'Husband's Relict'.[136]

The language of almost all inscriptions throughout the centuries renders the impression of a striking nationalization of the discourse on death and memory. Always being quite rare from the onset, Latin inscriptions hardly played a role any more on eighteenth- and nineteenth-century monuments. Only a small number of clerics was still commemorated in Latin after 1800 such as a Chaplain Coxe, who died in Arcot in 1820.[137] Instead, most inscriptions were now written in the native language of the deceased or of the political sovereign of the respective settlement. Against this backdrop, a quantitative analysis of the prevailing languages of inscriptions offers an elusive insight into cultural and political discourses as in the example of Danish Tranquebar.

The languages chosen for the inscriptions clearly reveal that Tranquebar—despite its Danish inhabitants—by no means was a mere Danish town around 1800 and even less during the nineteenth century. A number of Latin inscriptions renders evidence to the strong presence of the German–Danish missionaries who were mainly buried in the burial ground around the New Jerusalem Church. Even more striking is a large number of English inscriptions, which appear already during the 1760s. 49 English inscriptions are to be found on the cemeteries of Tranquebar from the period before 1920, in contrast to only 16 Danish inscriptions. The last Danish inscription dates back to 1850—only five years after Tranquebar had been ceded to the English East India Company. 17 Danes are commemorated by English texts, two of them already at the end of the eighteenth century, most of them since the 1840s. This is an obvious indicator for the fact that Tranquebar very soon after 1845 lost its Danish identity and was absorbed by ever-growing British India. The last Dane to die and to be buried in the Nyegade Kirkegaard facing the grey walls of the Danish fortress Dansborg was Arabella Due, who passed away on 26 June 1889 at the age of 68.[138]

NOTES

1. Rea, *Monumental Remains*, p. 44.
2. More, *Manual of the Trichinopoly District*, p. 50. Crole, *The Chingleput District*, p. 7. Carmichael, *Manual of the District of Vizagapatnam*, p. 29.
3. The Dutch sources mention the places 'Karreloer' and 'Arialcherry' near Sadras as major outlets for the production. See Peters, *In steen geschreven*, p. 133.
4. Ibid.
5. Rea, *Monumental Remains*, p. 44.
6. Ibid.
7. Compiled from the data given in Peters, *In steen geschreven*, chapter 'Begraafplaatsen langs de Kust Coromandel', pp. 149–232.
8. Compiled during own field studies in 2006. See under heading 'Inscriptions' in this chapter.
9. See, for example, the ledgers of Daniel and Sophia Massis (1658–65) and of Nicolaus Basly (1676) in the Dutch cemetery at Malacca.
10. Almost identical decorations and characters of inscriptions are to be found for Madras from around 1700–1, whose border-decorations are almost identical. These are the ledgers commemorating Ann Mary Parham, Anne Stubs, Francis Bett, Francis Ellis, and William Brooke. For the 1720s: The ledgers commemorating Stephen Barry, Samuel Brown, Edward Brooks, and John Cotterell.
11. Similarities are, for example, to be found on the ledgers of Anne Seaton (St. Mary's, 1691) and Catherine Whit as well as William Hamilton (St. John's, 1701, 1717); or of Hannah Seaton (St. Mary's, 1710) and Jonathan White (St. John's 1703); or of Stephen Baring, Samuel Brown (St. Mary's, 1719, 1720) and Mary Wallis, Elizabeth Cooper as well as Margery Jones (St. John's, 1718, 1719, 1723).
12. Despatch, 10 March 1681/2, see Penny, *Church in Madras*, vol. 1, p. 91.
13. St. Mary's Church, Vestry Proceedings, 24 March 1791, see ibid., p. 396.
14. Warren and Barlow, *St. Mary's Church*, pp. 140f. Groseclose, *British Sculpture and the Company Raj*, p. 52.
15. See, for example, the monument for the missionary Gericke (d. 1803) in St. Mary's Church, Fort St. George. Penny, *Church in Madras*, vol. 1, p. 503.
16. Wilkinson, *Two Monsoons*, pp. 15f.
17. Penny, *Church in Madras*, vol. 1, p. 580.
18. Furber, *Rival Empires*, pp. 289–97.
19. Between 1785 and 1789, the Rev. B. Millingchamp held the office of the

undertaker; until 1794 it was held by Andrew Bell, and between 1794 and 1805 by R.H. Kerr. See Penny, *Church in Madras*, vol. 2, p. 374.
20. Ibid.
21. See Drost, Tod und Erinnerung, passim.
22. See the *Madras Almanac and Compendium* (Madras Commercial List) from 1835.
23. Chennai Online, 2001, [www.chennaionline.com/cityfeature/fenn.asp].
24. The census of Tranquebar of 1790, for example, mentions a number of stone-masons residing there. See RA, Det kgl. Ostindiske Guvernement, 1747a, Mandtal over Indbyggerne i Tranquebar og Landsbyerne, 1790.
25. For example, one epitaph in St. Andrew's Church, Singapore, was produced by Llevellyn & Co., while quite a large number of inscription-plaques survives on Fort Canning Hill Cemetery, Singapore, carved by Llevellyn & Co. (1827–63), but also by Brown & Co. (1863), A.M. Carapiet (1834), Holmes & Co. (1851), H. Kyte (1832, 1835), Lindeman & Sons (1834, 1845), Murdock (1857), Simpson & Co. (1828) and J. Weaver (1838–9) from Calcutta. An investigation of these inscriptions leaves the impression that the better qualities were imported from Calcutta, while the local Singaporean produce was performed less sophisticated. Personal field studies in Singapore in January 2007. See also, Harfield, *Malacca*, pp. 55 ff. The memorial for William Charles (1847) on St. Paul's Hill Cemetery in Malacca, produced by Ostheider in Madras, proves to be the only exception.
26. Cooke, *Vizagapatnam and Waltair*, pp. 349–54.
27. Mors Janua Vitae Cemetery Vizagapatnam (number of inscriptions 1827–63): Madras 9, Calcutta 3, Bellary 1, N.N. 2; Flagstaff Cemetery Bimunipatnam (inscriptions 1835–1916): Calcutta 10, Madras 7, London 2, Thiruchirapalli 1, Vizagapatnam 1. See Cooke, *Vizagapatnam and Waltair*.
28. Francis, *The Nilgiris*, pp. 230–2.
29. For example, the weight of the stone-slab commemorating Montague Dundas Cockburn (died 28 September 1869) on the European cemetery at Kotagiri amounts to 620 kg.
30. British Library, Add. Mss. 45581–45653, Blechynden Papers: Diaries 1791–1822.
31. Allan & Co.; James Coull; J. Furlong; Hill & Co.; Hurst & Co.; Charlotte Sarah Law; John Law; E. Leggett; Ostheider & Co.; Charles de Rozario.
32. Mutiah, *Madras Rediscovered*, pp. 48–69.
33. Clemendez, Burton & Co.; Fitzgerald & Brothers; Horgan & Co.; Regel & Co.; Elizabeth De Sena; Thomas De Sena.

34. G.B. Bruce & Co.; Green & Co.; H.J. Revis (until 1855); Trotter & Co.
35. Gordon & Revis; H.J. Revis (from 1856).
36. J. Bennett; J.C. Fitzgerald.
37. Lawson, *Memories of Madras*, p. 274.
38. *Madras Almanac and Compendium*, 1846.
39. Chennai Online, 2001 [www.chennaionline.com/cityfeature/fenn.asp].
40. E.M. Lander, Kensal Green, London W, two inscriptions on Flagstaff Cemetery, Bimunipatnam (1873, 1912); Cox Buckley & Co., London, one inscription on Zion Church Cemetery, Tranquebar (1891); Barker & Son, Brompton Cemetery (St. Stephen's, Ootacamund, 1885); Burke, 144 Regent Street (St. Stephen's, Ootacamund, 1865).
41. William Augustus Asher, March 1921.
42. For example, in 1841 the Trustees of St. George's Cathedral informed the secretary of the government: 'We have the honour to state for the information of the Right Honorable the Governor in Council, that we have received a letter from Messrs. Arbuthnot and Co. requesting permission to erect in St. George's Cathedral, a Tablet to the Memory of the late Captain John Maitland Ross of the 5th Regiment Madras Native Infantry'. On the Arbuthnots, see Lawson, *Memoirs of Madras*, pp. 273–89, quotation from p. 281. 'We have inspected the tablet now lying at the office of Messrs. Arbuthnot and Co. and recommend that its erection in the Cathedral be sanctioned [. . .]'. IOR, 333/77, Ecclesiastical Department, 1841.
43. Lawson, *Memories of Madras*, p. 274.
44. *Deccan Herald* (online version), Metro Life, 26 August 2004.
45. Mutiah, *Madras Rediscovered*, pp. 85, 377.
46. Chennai Online, 2001 [www.chennaionline.com/cityfeature/fenn.asp].
47. Peters, *In steen geschreven*, p. 109.
48. Ibid., p. 225.
49. Ariès, *Geschichte des Todes*, p. 306.
50. Ibid., p. 307.
51. See regarding Portugal: Flor, *Tomb of the Noronha Family*, pp. 273–5.
52. Stephen, *Portuguese in the Tamil Coast*, p. 313.
53. Quoted after Ariès, *Geschichte des Todes*, p. 64.
54. Cotton, *List of Inscriptions*, p. 273.
55. Hosten, *Two Portuguese Inscriptions*. See also Stephen, *Portuguese in the Tamil Coast*, p. 313.
56. Kryger/Gasparski, *Tranquebar*, pp. 145–7. Peters, *In steen geschreven*, p. 199.
57. Kalpana/Schiffer, *Madras*, p. 271.
58. Bowrey, *Geographical Account*, p. 12.
59. Pereira, *Churches of Goa*, pp. 63–7.

60. Israel, *Dutch Republic*, pp. 637–45.
61. North, *Koloniale Kunstwelten*, pp. 59–67.
62. Ibid.
63. Ibid.
64. See, for example, the print 'Gravdelvers in de Grote Kerk' of J.C. Philips (1763), in De Vries, *Graven in de Grote of Sint-Bavokerk*, p. 14.
65. Schölvinck, *Graven in de Nieuwe Kerk*, p. 13.
66. Ibid., p. 19.
67. See beginning of this chapter.
68. Furber, *Rival Empires*, pp. 157–62.
69. See beginning of this chapter.
70. However, only a small number of monuments from this cemetery survives. See Peters, *In steen geschreven*, pp. 130f.
71. Ibid., p. 124.
72. See for example, the sketch of Tranquebar from 1723 (Copenhagen, Royal Library, NkS, 2168, folio), printed in Gøbel, *Jens Mortensen Sveigaards Ostindiske Rejsebeskrivelse*, p. 107. The outlines of fortress Dansborg likewise featured the reverse side of some seventeenth-century Indo–Danish coins. See Jensen, *Dansk Ostindien*, pp. 13f.
73. Quoted after Bowrey, *Geographical Account*, p. 52.
74. See, for example, Dutch shelf from *c*. 1635, which is preserved in the Frans Hals Museum at Haarlem.
75. Rea, *Monumental Remains*, p. 44.
76. Houlbrooke, *Death, Religion and Family in England*, p. 350.
77. Mytum, *Recording and Analysing*, p. 10.
78. See, for example, the ledgers of John Cornish (d. 1664), Nathaniel Foxcroft (d. 1670), Francesco Rodrigues Marques (d. 1687), Ann Meverell (d. 1689) and Bernard Midon (d. 1689).
79. Hallam/Hockey, *Death, Memory and Material Culture*, p. 54.
80. Ibid., pp. 54–68.
81. Mytum, *Recording and Analysing*, pp. 29f.
82. Peters, *In steen geschreven*, pp. 130f.
83. Quoted after Penny, *Church in Madras*, vol. 1, pp. 132, 374; vol. 2, p. 60.
84. All the more, at the beginning of the eighteenth century, the VOC felt compelled prohibiting the creation of monuments worth more than 200 pagodas. This fact may be seen as a clear indicator, that tremendously expensive monuments were quite common already during the seventeenth century, which—according to the contemporary perception—rather resembled Hindu or Muslim shrines than Christian funerary monuments: . . . dat niemant eenige grafsteden sal mogen laten maecken, meerder

kostende als twee hondert roepia's'. Quoted after Peters, *In steen geschreven*, p. 112.

85. Memmesheimer, *Das klassizistische Grabmal*, pp. 127–33.
86. See, for example, the Delft-fayences in the Netherlandish Rijksmuseum at Amsterdam.
87. Memmesheimer, *Das klassizistische Grabmal*, pp. 127–33.
88. Curl, *Death and Architecture*, pp. 168–87.
89. Ibid., pp. 171f.
90. Curl, *Victorian Celebration of Death*, p. 30.
91. Ibid., pp. 29f.
92. See Kryger/Gasparksi, *Tranquebar*, p. 16, picture 9.
93. Colvin, *Architecture and the After-Life*, p. 373.
94. Ibid., pp. 329–31.
95. Winckelmann, *Gedanken über die Nachahmung*.
96. See Curl, *Death and Architecture*, p. 142.
97. Colvin, *Architecture and the After-Life*, p. 332.
98. Lessing, *Wie die Alten den Tod gebildet*, pp. 87-100. Bukdahl, *Wiedewelt*, pp. 26–36.
99. At Cochin, only a few inscription-plates survive on the quite numerous monuments, so that a classification proves to be difficult.
100. Khan, *South Park Street Cemetery*, pp. 9f.
101. Kryger/Gasparski, *Tranquebar*, p. 156.
102. Kryger, *Nogle gravmæler i Dansk Ostindien – og et par stykker i København*, p. 274.
103. A similar tumba with sarcophagus is also to be found at the Nyegade Kirkegaard at Tranquebar (Joshua Mathias Kitson, child, d. 1800), see Kryger/Gasparski, *Tranquebar*, pp. 33f.
104. Colvin, *Architecture and the After-Life*, p. 370.
105. Curl, *Death and Architecture*, p. 157.
106. Dalrymple, *White Mughals*, pp. 138f.
107. Stephen, *Urbanism and the Chequered Existence*, p. 50.
108. See the monument of Samuel Thomasz (d.1808) at the Dutch Cemetery of Cochin.
109. Colvin, *Architecture and the After-Life*, p. 338, picture 314.
110. Krieger, *Kaufleute, Seeräuber und Diplomaten*, p. 145.
111. Maria Angelique Bech and Anna Maria Bech (d. 1816 and 1820), William Macleod (d. 1819), families Meinhardt and Borgen (d. 1804, 1807, 1810).
112. Willoughby Carpenter Stevenson (d. 1832), Anton Wilhelm Frederich Ruhde (d. 1832), Albert Reuben Augustus Godfrey (d. 1846), Theodora

Clara Due (d. 1847), Christopher Eibye (d. 1849), P.H.K. Wodschow (d. 1857).

113. Margaret Lloyd (d. 1820), families Klein and Kofoed (d. 1841, 1854 and 1876), M.E. Halkier (d. 1865).
114. Kryger/Gasparski, *Tranquebar*, pp. 137–41. Kryger/Gasparski attribute the monument to Matthias Jürgen Mühldorff (d. 1836).
115. Kryger/Gasparski, *Tranquebar*, pp. 24–6.
116. Curl, *Death and Architecture*, p. 249.
117. Both having died in 1882 and 1867 respectively.
118. See below in this chapter.
119. Colvin, *Architecture and the After-Life*, p. 373.
120. Francis, *Nilgiris*, p. 183.
121. Memmesheimer, *Das klassizistische Grabmal*, pp. 92–103.
122. Olivia Adelaide Petersen (d. 1854), William Christian Petersen (d. 1860). See Kryger/Gasparski, *Tranquebar*, p. 89.
123. Francis, *South Arcot*, p. 280.
124. Houlbrooke, *Death, Religion, and the Family in England*, p. 363.
125. Mytum, *Recording and Analysing*, p. 12.
126. Ibid., pp. 36–9.
127. See, for example, Howard and Sarah Dowker and Frederick Spencer Pope in St. Stephen's Churchyard, Ootacamund.
128. Quoted after Curl, *Death and Architecture*, p. 250.
129. For a cultural history of tomb-inscriptions see the study of Karl S. Guthke, *Sprechende Steine*.
130. Ariès, *Geschichte des Todes*, p. 67.
131. Ibid.
132. Richard Brathwayte, *Remains after Death, Including by Way of Introduction Divers Memorable Observances Occasioned upon Discourse of Epitaphs and Epycedes*, London 1618; see Guthke, *Sprechende Steine*, p. 54.
133. Guthke, *Sprechende Steine*, p. 12.
134. Ibid., passim.
135. Ibid., p. 48.
136. Monument George and Jane Boddrey 1869–70, St. Mary's Cemetery, Madras.
137. Penny, *Church in Madras*, vol. 1, p. 129.
138. Evidence regarding the languages on the tomb monuments derives from the author's own field studies as well as from Kryger/Gasparski, *Tranquebar*.

CHAPTER 4

Conclusion

EUROPEAN CEMETERIES: AN UNDERESTIMATED ASSET?

Walking across St. Stephen's Cemetery at Ootacamund still sends a slight 'shudder' down the spire similar to Francis Burton's impressions when he visited this place during the 1840s. The straight footpaths and stairs guiding our view from the church below towards the mountains remain almost unchanged. Even the traffic noise, which sprawls out from the nearby street, hardly disturbs the sense of time long past, which seems to have survived at this place. In some distance from Ootacamund, we reach the forgotten European burial ground at Kotagiri clinging up a steep slope and surrounded by lush tea gardens. Hardly any locals and even less tourists visit this place, which accommodates the earliest surviving European tomb-monuments of the Nilgiris from the 1820s. Nobody really takes care of the ensemble, and the site is likely to disappear in the coming decades. In the plains, most European burial grounds are situated inside the growing towns. With shortage of space everywhere, European cemeteries are often being pulled down or misused as public latrines, etc. Visiting St. Mary's Cemetery in Madras is as disgusting as walking across formerly Dutch 'Karikop' of Nagapattinam (which is full of snakes) or the almost entirely destroyed British cemetery of Cuddalore.

Only in a few instances, the grounds are still protected, as in the case of St. George's Cemetery in Madurai or the recently renovated burial grounds at formerly Danish Tranquebar. In Tranquebar, the Nyegade Kirkegaard as well as the graves around New Jerusalem Church and Zion Church contribute to the unique historical appearance of that town. Tranquebar stands apart from the most dynamic centres of economic development in Tamil Nadu, which has obviously saved the architectural heritage of the past decades. Here, European as well as Indian town architecture is increasingly perceived as a tourist attraction. The same applies to the remaining ledgers of the old Guava Garden at Fort St. George, which survive around St. Mary's Church in Madras.

More than six decades have passed since the end of the British Raj, and about half a century since the British debates on the abandonment of the European cemeteries in India. While only little attention has been paid on this issue from the European side ever since, the Indian people have chosen different approaches towards this European material heritage on the subcontinent: from neglect to full preservation and establishment of heritage sites. Today, the times of colonial and imperial discourses have faded away and render space for more pragmatic deliberations on the future of the European burial grounds in India. It is obvious that the Indian societies, even the Christian churches in India, are not in a position or feel the need of maintaining the European tomb-monuments. Facing about 1,350 surviving sites throughtout entire India, it seems to be futile to claim funds from Europe for renovation of all of them. The most feasible way still seems to let most grounds to 'revert to nature' as was stipulated during the 1940s and 1950s. However, even this should be carried out in a respectful manner rather than misusing them as public toilets or as store houses for building materials like stones or metals. Even this seems to be a difficult task today. Nevertheless, many burial grounds need to be protected as historical heritage sites. While some Dutch, Danish, French and the very few Portuguese monuments are already looked after and protected, the abundant British funerary heritage remains largely neglected.

A touristic heritage scheme may include a better protection of a number of cemeteries in south India such as the following sites:

- the St. Mary's Cemetery at Madras
- the Kilpauk Cemetery at Madras (a beautiful garden-cemetery with, however, very few remaining European monuments)
- the British and French portions of the cemetery at Cholas Nagar in Pondicherry

- the few remaining ledgers at Cuddalore
- the Dutch burial ground at Porto Novo/Parangipettai
- the Karikop at Nagapattinam
- the St. George's Cemetery at Madurai
- the St. Stephen's Church Cemetery at Ootacamund
- the 'European Cemetery' at Kotagiri
- the British cemetery at Seringapatam
- the Dutch cemetery at Cochin

Notably, Parangipettai and Kotagiri seem to be in the most precarious condition. An official status as a heritage site might yield further protection from vandalism and disturbance. At least new gates with watchmen and proper walls are in demand.

Today, tourism constitutes a major and ever increasing source of income for India. Even if we know that the European cemeteries in India cannot compete with thousands of outstanding temples and palaces, they may complement the spectrum of tourist sites in the future. Many Europeans are regularly in search of their ancestor's graves in India. Name lists like those provided by FIBIS can facilitate an easy approach and identification of graves. Furthermore, maps of the location of the burial grounds are needed, for most of them are situated in remote places and are difficult to find. Establishing historical burial grounds as tourist heritage spots in remote areas, which are not touched by foreign tourism, can attract tourists to those regions. Hotels and restaurants will benefit by the integration of European burial grounds into tourist schemes. Tranquebar again renders a good example for the success of such projects. However, which foreign tourist has ever visited Parangipettai or Nagapattinam?

Hopefully, this small volume will achieve its major goal to highlight the unique historical significance of the European cemeteries in south India. More exhaustive studies will be needed to record and study the thousands of monuments from before 1947. Nostalgia or ideological approaches may not be feasible channels to handle this heritage. Even today's romantic eye cannot conceal the fact that India was chiefly an object of enrichment and domination for the Europeans. Nevertheless, behind this broader frame of

Company policy lies a sphere of private desire, hope and despair. A walk across one of the forgotten European cemeteries with their evidence for early death, personal grief and mourning may well yield a much clearer insight into the unknown side of European life in India.

Bibliography

SOURCES

INDIA OFFICE RECORDS, LONDON (IOR)

N/2, Ecclesiastical Returns Madras, 1698–1740.
N/3, Madras Ecclesiastical Consultations, 1730–1798.
N/5, Madras Wills, Administrations and Inventories, 1790–1840.
R/4, British High Commission Cemetery Records, *c*. 1870–1967.
333/77, Ecclesiastical Department, 1840.

RIGSARKIVET KØBENHAVN (DANISH NATIONAL ARCHIVES) (RA)

Asiatisk Kompagni, 1770a, Zions Kirkes og fattigkasses regnskaber 1781–1817.
Det kgl. Ostindiske Guvernement, 1747a, Mandtal over Indbyggerne i Tranquebar og Landsbyerne, 1790.

HANDELS-OG SØFARTSMUSSET PAA KRONBORG (DENMARK)

Knud Heiberg, Afskrifter af indskrifterne i Tranquebar med personalhistoriske noter, 1935.

LANDSARKIVET FOR SJÆLLAND, LOLLAND-FALSTER & BORNHOLM, COPENHAGEN

Sogn Nr. 777, Tranquebar Zions Kirkebog, 1767–1845 (microfiche).

ARCHIV DER BRÜDER-UNITÄT HERRNHUT (ARCHIVES OF THE MORAVIAN BRETHREN HERRNHUT) (UAH)

R15 Ta No. 1.7, Reiß Diarium 1755–1756.

PRINTED SOURCE MATERIAL

Beavan, H., *Thirty Years in India: Or, a Soldier's Reminiscences of Native and European Life in the Presidencies, from 1808 to 1838*, vol. 2, London, 1839.
Boswell, A. John, *A Manual of the Nellore District in the Presidency of Madras*, Madras, 1873.
Bowrey, Thomas, *A Geographical Account of Countries Round the Bay of Bengal*,

1669 to 1679, ed. Richard Carnac Temple, London 1905, rpt. New Delhi, 1997.

Burton, Richard F., *Goa, and the Blue Mountains: Or Six Months of Sick Leave*, New Delhi, 2003, p. 183.

Cooke, David, *Bimlipatnam: Christian Cemeteries* (BACSA Cemetery Records), London, 1988.

———, *Vizagapatnam and Waltair* (BACSA Cemetery Records), London, 1992.

———, *Vizianagaram: Cantonment Cemetery* (BACSA Cemetery Records), London, 1988.

Cotton, Julian James, *List of Inscriptions on Tombs or Monuments in Madras Possessing Historical or Archaeological Interest*, Madras, 1905.

Crole, Charles Steward, *The Chingleput, late Madras, District. A Manual compiled under the orders of the Madras Government*, Madras, 1879.

de Jong, Peter, *Quilon and Trivandrum* (BASCA Cemetery Records), London, 1992.

De Rozario, M., *The Complete Monumental Register: Containing all the Epitaphs, inscriptions, &c. &c. &c. in the different churches and burial grounds, in and about Calcutta; including those of the burial grounds of Howrah. . . . Together with several inscriptions from the presidencies of Madras, Bombay, Isle of France, & c. To which is added short sketches, anecdotes, &c. &c. illustrative of the public services, general characters, and virtues of the dead*, Calcutta, 1815.

Dickens, Charles, All The Year Round: A Weekly Journal, vol. 10, 29 August 1863–6 February 1864. (*Something to be done in India*, pp. 103–7).

Gøbel, Erik (ed.), *Jens Mortensen Sveigaards ostindiske reijsebeskrivelse, 1665–84*, [Maritim Kontakt, vol. 27], Copenhagen, 2005, p. 90.

Gründler, Johann Ernst, *Malabarischer Medicus, welcher kurtzen Bericht giebet, theils was diese Heyden in der Medicin vor Principia haben; theils auf was Art und mit welchen Medikamenten sie die kranckheiten curieren. Denen Herren medicis in Europe zu dienlicher Nachricht aus denen Medicinischen Büchern der Malabaren zusammen getragen und über setzet* [. . .], manuscript, 1711 [Archive of the Francken's Foundation, Halle].

Harfield, Alan, *Christian Cemeteries and Memorials in the State of Malacca* (BACSA Cemetery Records), London, 2002.

Hawkesworth, John, *Asiaticus. Part the first: Ecclesiastical and Historical Sketches Respecting Bengal. Part the Second: The Epitaphs in the Different Burial Grounds in and about Calcutta*, Calcutta, 1803.

Holmes and Co., *Bengal Obituary: Or a Record to Perpetuate the Memory of the Departed Worth*, Calcutta, 1851.

Hull, Edmund C.P., *The European in India: Or Anglo-Indian's Vade-Mecum*, London, 1878 (rpt. New Delhi-Chennai, 2004).

Kipling, Rudyard, *Something of Myself: For My Friends Known and Unknown*, London, 1937 (rpt. New Delhi, 1997).

Lessing, Gotthold Ephraim, *Wie die Alten den Tod gebildet. Eine Untersuchung*, Berlin, 1769 (rpt. Stuttgart, 1984).

Madras Almanac and Compendium of Intelligence, Madras, 1835–70.

Malden, C.H., *List of Burials at Madras from 1680 to 1746 compiled from the Register of St. Mary's Church, Fort St. George*, Madras, 1903.

More, Lewis, *Manual of the Trichinopoly District in the Presidency of Madras*, Madras, 1878.

The Parliamentary Debate (HANSARD), Fifth Series, volume CLXI, House of Lords, Official Report, Third Volume of Session 1948–49, London, 1949.

Platt, Kate, *The Home and Health in India and the Tropical Colonies*, London, 1923.

Price, J. Frederick et al. (eds), *The Private Diary of Ananda Ranga Pillai*, 12 vols., Madras, 1904–28.

Rea, Alexander, *Monumental Remains of the Dutch East India Company in the Presidency of Madras* (Archaeological Survey of India, New Imperial Series, vol. 25), Madras 1897, (rpt. New Delhi, 1998).

Spectator, no. 26, 30 March 1711.

Urquhart, William, *The Oriental Obituary . . . being an impartial compilation from monumental inscriptions on the tombs of those persons whose ashes were deposited in remote parts . . . since the formation of European Settlements, to the present time. To which is added Biographical Sketches, Anecdotes, etc.*, 3 vols., Madras 1809.

Winckelmann, Johann Joachim, *Gedanken über die Nachahmung der griechischen Werke in der Malerey und Bildhauerkunst*, Jena, 1755, (Engl tr. *Reflections on the Painting and Sculpture of the Greeks. With Instructions for the Connoisseur and an Essay on Grace in Works of Art*, London, 1765).

ONLINE RESOURCES

Chennai Online, 2001 [www.chennaionline.com/cityfeature/fenn.asp].

Deccan Herald (online version), Metro Life, 26 August 2004.

LITERATURE

Ariès, Philippe, *Geschichte des Todes*, 11th edn., Munich, 2005.

Bacci, Massimo Livi, Introduction, in: Alain Bideau, Bertrand Besjardins, Héctor

Pérez Brignoli (eds.), *Infant and Child Mortality in the Past*, Oxford 1997, pp. 1–3.

Banerjea, Dhrubajyoti, *European Calcutta: Images and Recollections of a Bygone Era*, 3rd edn., New Delhi, 2008.

Buettner, Elizabeth, *Empire Families: Britons and Late Imperial India*, Oxford, 2005.

Bukdahl, Else Marie, *Johannes Wiedewelt. From Winckelmann's Vision of Antiquity to Sculptural Concepts of the 1980s*, Hellerup, 1993.

Carmichael, D. (ed.), *A Manual of the District of Vizagpatnam in the Presidency of Madras*, Madras, 1869.

Chadha, Ashish, 'Ambivalent Heritage: Between Affect and Ideology in a Colonial Cemetery', *Journal of Material Culture*, 11, 3 (2006), pp. 339–63.

Church of South India (ed.), *St. Mary's Church*, Madras, 1996.

Colvin, Howard, *Architecture and the After-Life*, New Haven-London, 1991.

Curl, James Stevens, *The Victorian Celebration of Death*, Phoenix Mill Thrupp, Stroud, Gloucestershire, 2000.

———, *Death and Architecture: An Introduction to Funerary and Commemorative Buildings in the Western European Tradition, with some Considerations of their Settings*, Phoenix Mill Thrupp, Stroud, Gloucestershire, 2002.

Dalrymple, William, *White Mughals: Love and Betrayal in Eighteenth-Century India*, New Delhi, 2004.

Deloche, Jean, *Senji (Gingee): A Fortified City in the Tamil Country*, Pondicherry, 2005.

Drost, Alexander, *Tod und Erinnerung in der kolonialen Gesellschaft. Koloniale Sepulkralkultur in Bengalen (17. and 19. Jahrhundert)*, Jena 2011.

Dyson, Tim (ed.), *India's Historical Demography: Studies in Famine, Disease and Society*, London 1989.

Dyson, Tim, 'Infant and Child Mortality in the Indian Subcontinent, 1881–1947', in Alain Bideau, Bertrand Besjardins, Héctor Pérez Brignoli (eds.), *Infant and Child Mortality in the Past*, Oxford, 1997, pp. 109–34.

Flor, Pedro, 'The Tomb of the Noronha Family and Funerary Renaissance Sculpture in Portugal', in Barbara Borngässer, Henrik Karge and Bruno Klein (eds.), *Grabkunst und Sepulkralkultur in Spanien und Portugal / Arte funerario y culture sepulchral en España y Portugal*, Hamburg, 2006, pp. 273–86.

Francis, W., *The Nilgiris* [Madras District Gazetteers], Madras, 1908 (rpt. New Delhi, 2001).

Fuhring, Peter, *Ornament in Prent: Zeventiende-eeuwse ornamentprenten in de verzamelingen van het Rijksmuseum (Ornament in Print; Seventeenth*

Century Ornament Prints in the Collections of the Rijksmuseum), Amsterdam, 1998.

Furber, Holden, *Rival Empires of Trade in the Orient 1600–1800*, Minneapolis, 1976.

Glaser, Rüdiger, Stefan Militzer and Rory Walsh, 'Weather and Climate at Madras, India, in the Years 1732–1737 Based Upon an Analysis of the Weather Diary of the German Missionary Geisler', in *Würzburger Geographische Arbeiten*, vol. 80, 1991, pp. 45–86.

Grove, Richard H. and John Chappell, 'El Niño: Chronology and the History of Global Crises during the Little Ice Age', in Richard H. Grove and John Chappell (eds.), *El Niño—History and Crisis: Studies from the Asia-Pacific Region*, Cambridge 2000, pp. 5–33.

Guthke, Karl S., *Epitaph Culture in the West*, Cambridge 2003.

———, *Sprechende Steine. Eine Kulturgeschichte der Grabschrift*, Göttingen, 2006.

Hallam, Elizabeth and Jenny Hockey, *Death, Memory and Material Culture*, Oxford, New York, 2001.

Hosten, Henry, 'Two Portuguese Inscriptions in the Kapaleeswarar Temple, Mailapur (Madras)', in *Journal of the Asiatic Society of Bengal*, New series, vol. IX, 4, 1913, pp. 169–71.

Houlbrooke, Ralph, *Death, Religion, and the Family in England, 1480–1750*, (2nd edn.), Oxford, 2000.

Israel, Jonathan I., *Dutch Primacy in World Trade, 1585–1740*, Oxford, 1989.

———, *The Dutch Republic: Its Rise, Greatness, and Fall. 1477–1806*, Oxford, 1998.

Jensen, Uno Barner, *Dansk Ostindien: Handelsmønter og mønterne fra Trankebar*, Brovst, 1996.

Kalpana, K. and Frank Schiffer, *Madras: The Architectural Heritage*, Chennai, 2003.

Khan, Aurelius, *The South Park Street Cemetery Calcutta*, Calcutta, 1997.

Krieger, Martin, *Kaufleute, Seeräuber und Diplomaten. Der dänische Handel auf dem Indischen Ozean (1620–1868)*, Cologne-Weimar-Vienna, 1998.

———, 'Koloniale Wohnkultur an der Koromandelküste zwischen 17. und 19. Jahrhundert: Von der Faktorei-Epoche zur territorialen Expansion', in Michael North (ed.), *Kultureller Austausch: Bilanz und Perspektiven der Frühneuzeitforschung*, Köln-Weimar-Wien, 2009, pp. 409–30.

Kryger, Karin and Lisbeth Gasparski, *Tranquebar: Kirkegårde og Gravminder. Med personalhistoriske noter ved Knud Heiberg*, Copenhagen, 2002.

Kulke, Hermann and Dietmar Rothermund, *Geschichte Indiens. Von der Induskultur bis heute* (2nd edn.), Munich, 1998.

Labouvie, Eva, *Andere Umstände. Eine Kulturgeschichte der Geburt*, Cologne-Weimar-Vienna, 1998.

Lawson, Charles, *Memories of Madras*, London, 1905 (rpt. New Delhi, 2002).

Love, Henry Davidson, *Vestiges of Old Madras 1640–1800. Traced from the East India Company's Records preserved at Fort St. George and the India Office, and from other Sources*, vol. 3, London, 1913.

Memmesheimer, Paul Arthur, *Das klassizistische Grabmal. Eine Typologie*, diss.-phil., Bonn, 1969.

Mentz, Søren, *The English Gentleman Merchant at Work: Madras and the City of London 1660–1740*, Copenhagen, 2005.

Mutiah, S., *Madras Rediscovered: A Historical Guide to Looking Around, supplemented with Tales of 'Once upon a City'*, Chennai-Bangalore-Hyderabad, 1999.

Mytum, Harold, *Recording and Analysing Graveyards* [Practical Handbooks in Archaeology, no. 15], Walmgate, York, 2000.

Nilsson, Sten, *European Architecutre in India 1750–1850*, London, 1968.

North, Michael, 'Koloniale Kunstwelten in Ostindien. Kulturelle Kommunikation im Umkreis der Handelskompanien', in *Jahrbuch für europäische Überseegeschichte*, vol. 5, 2005, pp. 55–72.

Penny, Frank, *The Church in Madras: Being the History of the Ecclesiastical and Missionary Action of the East India Company in the Presidency of Madras in the Seventeenth and Eighteenth Centuries*, 2 vols., London, 1904–12.

Pereira, José, *Churches of Goa*, New Delhi, 2003.

Perrenoud, Alfred, 'Child Mortality in Francophone Europe: State of Knowledge', in Alain Bideau, Bertrand Besjardins, Héctor Pérez Brignoli (eds.), *Infant and Child Mortality in the Past*, Oxford, 1997, pp. 22–37.

Peters, Marion, *In steen geschreven: Leven en sterven van VOC-dienaren op de Kust van Coromandel in India*, Amsterdam, 2002.

Raychaudhuri, Tapan, *Jan Company in Coromandel 1605–1696: A Study in the Interrelations of European Commerce and Traditional Economies*, The Hague, 1962.

Rea, Alexander, *Monumental Remains of the Dutch East India Company in the Presidency of Madras*, [Archaeological Survey of India, New Imperial Series, vol. 25], Madras 1897 (rpt. New Delhi–Madras, 1998).

Schölvinck, Hester, *Graven in de Nieuwe Kerk Amsterdam*, Amsterdam.

Shorters, Iola A., *A Wasting Historical Asset? A Comparative Study of Grave Memorials at Wootton Waven, King's Norton and Birmingham, c. 1700–1940*, Cambridge, 2004.

Srivastava, Harish C., 'Trends in Birth and Death Rates in Goa, 1820–1910: Some Evidence gathered from the Baptism and Burial Records of a Parish', in *Journal of Asian and African Studies*, vol. 22, ½ (January–April 1987), pp. 87–95.

Stephen, S. Jeyaseela, 'Urbanism and the Chequered Existence of the Indo-French Town of Pondicherry (A.D. 1674–1793)', in *Revue Historique de Pondichéry*, vol. 19, 1996, pp. 29–64.

———, *Portuguese in the Tamil Coast: Historical Explorations in Commerce and Culture (1507–1749)*, Pondicherry, 1998.

Subramanian, T.S., 'Unravelling a Dutch Past', *The Hindu*, Online edn., 14 August 2006.

Talboys Wheeler, J., *Madras in the Olden Time: Being a History of the Presidency from the first Foundation of Fort St. George to the Occupation of Madras by the French, 1639–1748*, Madras 1892 (rpt. New Delhi–Madras, 1998).

Thomlinson, Ralph, *Population Dynamics: Causes and Consequences of World Demographic Change*, New York, 1965.

Van Epen, D.G., 'Graf schriften in Voor-Indie', in *De Wapenheraut*, 1897, pp. 173–7, 201–9, 245–51.

Varghese, Nina, 'Will Pulicat Make it?', *The Hindu*. Business Line. Internet Edition, 6 August 2001.

Vries, Adriaan de, *Graven in de Grote of Sint-Bavokerk te Haarlem*, Haarlem, 2006.

Warren, W.H. and Barlow, N., *St. Mary's Church: A Brief History with a Description of its Monuments and other Objects of Interest with Illustrations and a Plan*, Madras, 1990.

Wilkinson, Theon, *Two Monsoons: The Life and Death of Europeans in India* (2nd edn.), London, 1987.

Woods, Robert, 'Infant Mortality in Britain. A Survey of Current Knowledge on Historical Trends and Variations', in Alain Bideau, Bertrand Besjardins, Héctor Pérez Brignoli (eds.), *Infant and Child Mortality in the Past*, Oxford, 1997, pp. 74–87.

Index of Names

Index of Place Names